WHAT IS HUMAN NATURE

A Brief Social-Psychological History of Our Species

David Weiner
Austin, Tx.

WHAT IS
HUMAN NATURE

A Brief Social-Psychological History of Our Species

David Weiner

Published By
Positive Imaging, LLC
bill@positive-imaging.com

ISBN: 9781951776725

Contents

Preface

This essay argues for optimism about the future, based on scholarly observation and research. This material is the core of my sociology classes. Students critique, discuss and debate it to enhance collaborative thinking as an avenue to understanding and wisdom. Most students have found the material illuminating. As a result of the class, many express a desire to engage in environmental activism.

Introduction

Human beings today are faced with challenges unlike any in our history. Our behavior in the near future will probably determine not only whether we continue to thrive on this planet, but whether many other species do so as well. How did we get into this fix? Can we, as a society, make the decisions necessary to create a positive outcome? This long essay addresses these questions, coming to the conclusion that a particular combination of innate human attributes provides reason for optimism. To make this argument involves integrating material from a number of disciplines.

The first segment of Part 14 contains a summary of this analysis. The reader may wish to begin there.

Section I: Our Egalitarian Origins

Part 1: Where We Came From

About fourteen billion years ago our universe was born. Nine billion years later the planet Earth materialized out of a gas cloud, and five billion years after that the first single-celled living organisms appeared on its rocky, volcanic surface. For many millions of years, through a process called evolution, simple single-celled organisms gave rise to complex single-celled organisms containing various parts. These, in turn, gave rise to multi-celled organisms, some of which evolved into complex creatures -- like us. Some of the early complex creatures began to live in communities of their own kind, and these communities took on a kind of organic quality, as if they were organisms themselves. Just as the different parts of a cell cooperated to make the cell survive, and just as the parts of a frog cooperated to allow the frog to survive, the members of a wolf community cooperated to enable the pack to survive.

Skipping ahead past early plants such as ferns and mosses, and animals including fish, reptiles, amphibians, and insects, to about two hundred million years ago, we find mammals— the biological class that humans belong to. Unlike insects, mammals had internal rather than external skeletons, and unlike reptiles, birds, and fish they mostly bore their offspring live rather than laid eggs. They mainly lived in groups, hunted and foraged cooperatively, and possessed a particularly large brain. It contained a powerful reasoning center called the cerebral cortex. Humans possess a cerebral cortex so advanced that it carries the label neo(new)cortex. When an extinction event wiped out most of the huge, often fierce, sometimes quite intelligent dinosaurs that roamed the planet about sixty-six million years ago, mammals ascended to the top of the food chain.

Mammals became a large class, containing a great variety of creatures including a particularly large-brained order called primates, composed of lemurs, monkeys, and apes. A particular family of apes called great apes, or hominids, had even larger brains than other primates. They also had better vision and hearing, hands and feet with flexible thumbs, and limber fingers and toes. This combination of attributes enabled them to extract nuts and fruits from hard-to-get-at places; to use sticks and stones as tools with which to crack nuts, dig up roots, get the honey out of beehives and invade termite nests; and also to kill and eat small animals. Most primates dined on plant life exclusively, but some hominids ate meat as well. They groomed one another constantly, which was their way of socializing, and lived in well-organized, kin-related bands.

Hominids originated in East Africa and were divided among two subfamilies. One of these contained the orangutans. The other included gorillas, chimpanzees, bonobos, and beginning about two million years ago, homos, or hominins — our ancestors. Hominins, unlike other hominids, were bipedal. They could stand erect and walk and run on two feet, rather than hunker along on four. This improved their visual grasp of any environment they wandered into. They may even have possessed some rudimentary language, which would have made cooperative hunting and foraging easier for them. Recent research suggests that just walking upright may have contributed to their developing larger brains, because of how much more difficult this was from a balancing point of view; and this, in turn, might have contributed to their development of language skills (*Scientific American*, September 2018).

Homo Erectus, our immediate ancestor, lived in bands of fifteen to thirty extended family, or clan members. They possessed larger brains than their ancestors and even better hands, allowing them to grasp and use tools with

greater facility and imagination. Perhaps most importantly, they could pick up tiny seeds. These traits and skills
vastly expanded the food sources available to hominins,
as well as extended the size of the areas they could
range in search of nourishment. Their hunting ability too
was more advanced. They could cooperate to herd and
trap antelope in canyons, capture buffalo and mastodons
in concealed pits, and employ well-designed spears and
lances to slaughter them.

Part 2: The Importance of Language

About three hundred thousand years ago, Homo erectus gave rise to two sub-species even more skilled at collaborative hunting. One was Homo sapien Neanderthalensis —Neanderthals—and the other was Homo sapien sapiens — also called anatomically modern humans: us. Scholars still debate the exact relationship between Neanderthals and modern humans (Haviland, 2011, Ch. 4). Many now feel that Neanderthals were close enough cousins that they should be called humans. Several other subspecies, such as Denisovans, were also present. No homos, however, were as numerous as modern humans and Neanderthals. All thrived together and almost certainly interbred. However, by thirty-thousand years ago only modern humans remained. An early hypothesis proposed that this was because a disease arose that killed everyone except themselves, who somehow possessed immunity to it. However, a more recent proposal, based on more advanced archeology, suggests a different explanation. In *Sapiens: A brief history of humankind* (2015), Historian, Yuval Harari asked,

What was the Sapiens' secret of success? How did we manage to settle so rapidly in so many distant and ecologically different habitats? How did we push all other human species into oblivion? Why couldn't even the strong, brainy, cold-proof Neanderthals survive our onslaught? The debate continues to rage. The most likely answer is the very thing that makes the debate possible. Homo sapiens conquered the world thanks above all to its unique language (Harari, 2015, p.19).

This happened between one hundred fifty-thousand, and seventy-thousand years ago. Perhaps, given more time, Neanderthals would have acquired advanced language, but this remains unknown. With the aid of their advanced communication skills, modern humans could hunt and gather more efficiently, form stronger bonds within their communities, and conduct warfare more effectively. In the final analysis, they simply annihilated all weaker communities who competed with them for resources.

However, until they developed language, our ancestors barely survived. Their big brains required a great deal of energy and the bulk of what they ate went into providing it. Hence, their musculature could not compare with that of most other predators. Until they discovered the benefits of fire, humans' survival depended heavily upon cracking open and sucking the marrow from bones left by lions and leopards, and the scavenging hyenas and jackals that followed after them. Using fire to cook food changed everything. Cooking, rendered meat and vegetables easier and faster to digest. Because raw food required so much more energy to digest, large nocturnal predators and scavengers had to sleep after feasting. While they slept, homos scavenged and hunted small animals at will. They also learned to use fire to keep large predators out of their campsites.

Edward O. Wilson, the founder of the field of research called Social Biology, deduced that cooking food also had an additional, enormous consequence for our species.

There is a growing consensus among paleontologists that the origin of our species — and the massive cerebral memory banks that define it — were forged in the firelight of African campsites. The impetus was the cooking of meat ... It led to the clustering of band members and gave advantage to conversation... Social intelligence became premium. ... From the earliest Homo formed, as brain size increased, the time devoted to social interactions likely increased.... In short, longer social interaction is a likely key component in the evolution of a larger brain and higher intelligence (Wilson, 2019, pp. 149-50).

The inventive genius of modern humans, combined with their ability to converse richly, made them the most diversified and skilled collaborators of all primates — and this gave them great power. Archeological evidence shows that, unlike Neanderthals and other homos, modern human hunting parties often included people from more than one band. These parties sometimes numbered in the hundreds, with everyone cooperating efficiently. Modern human bands could also join forces with others of their kind to confront a common enemy or deal with a natural disaster. Most bands contained mostly kin-related people, but quite often they contained non-kin-related members as well. This had far-reaching consequences. Bands speaking different languages and practicing different rituals, sometimes having fought with one another in the past, could collaborate at dealing with mutual threats and achieving mutual goals. No other creature could organize in such a fashion, and these skills greatly enhanced modern human thriving (Haviland, 2011, ch. 7; Boyd, 2018, ch. 2).

Part 3: The Power of Altruism

In addition to sophisticated language, modern humans possessed another trait to an advanced degree that enhanced their ability to collaborate effectively. This trait was altruism.

Webster's Collegiate Dictionary defines altruism as:
1: unselfish regard for or devotion to the welfare of others
2: behavior by an animal that is not beneficial to or may be harmful to itself but that benefits others of its species

In 1859, in *Origin of the Species*, Charles Darwin described how a process called *natural selection* enhanced the thriving of life forms. This became the basis for his theory of evolution. Nature selected beings with genes less well suited to the environment for extinction, when in competition with beings possessing better-suited genes. Only the latter survived. Individuals who belonged to species possessing genes that drove them to form cooperative communities fared better than loners. Therefore, Darwin reasoned, nature favored species and sub-species that cooperated the most efficiently and eliminated those that did not. The appearance of a gene for altruism, first among insects and then among other creatures, played an enormous role in promoting group survival based on cooperation. This occurred first among termites and ants.

The earliest known origins of eusocial [altruistic] colonies occurred in the termites, dating back to the Early Cretaceous period, about two hundred million years before the present. The termites were followed by the ants roughly fifty million years later, and the two together — the termites consuming dead vegetation and the ants consuming termites and other small prey, thereafter came to dominate the ecology of the insect world (Wilson 2019, p. 44).

Wilson went on to document how every time altruism, a trait that rarely appeared in nature, became established among a species, that species rose to dominance.

However, altruism always had to compete with another genetic drive: individuals' urge to reproduce only their genes and to disable other members of their species from doing the same.

The potential competition of individual versus group pervades all levels of life, from cells to empires. The conflicts they generate fill the textbooks of the social sciences, and they endlessly enrich the humanities. Restraint and altruism resist scientific explanation because they seem at first so difficult to achieve by biologically evolving populations. To spread, they must impose at each level of biological organization from cell to society a powerful counterforce of natural selection against the 'ordinary' natural selection already in place... The group, for example, must overcome the regency of the organism and the seeming absolute priority of selfish personal success (Wilson 1975, pp. 57-8).

Altruism genes, then, urged one to support others, despite one's drive to diminish others in service of one's own selfish needs. As it turned out, however, by doing so altruism actually enhanced one's ability to pass along one's genes to a future generation. In 1989, Richard Dawkins published *The Selfish Gene*, which became an immediate bestseller. It explained in simple terms how altruism works. Whether or not one consciously wishes to sacrifice personal goals in favor of community needs, the genes comprising one's DNA possess a strong desire to do so, and influence one's choices without one being aware of it. These genes "know" that the cousins of oneself all carry a version of themselves. If oneself is a good warrior, then one should fight and risk death, thus to ensure that some of the cousins of oneself survive, even if oneself does not. In this manner, one's genes will survive, hence one's species will live on -- even though one-self is dead. If one refuses to fight, the annihilation of one's community, one's band, even one's species, becomes more likely. This kind of altruism carries the label kin-based or inclusive-fitness altruism.

But what if the members of an individual's group were not kin related? E.O. Wilson initially assumed that human bands were usually kin-related because this kind of social organization maximized gene-based motivation to cooperate with others. Subsequent research showed, however, that even when members of human bands (and some other animal communities as well) were not related they still practiced inclusive-fitness altruism through a variation that evolutionary biologists labeled reciprocal altruism:

The theory of reciprocal altruism states that adaptations for providing benefits to non-relatives can evolve as long as the delivery of such benefits is reciprocated at some point in the future. ... Those who engage in reciprocal altruism will tend to out-reproduce those who act selfishly, causing psychological mechanisms for reciprocal altruism to spread in succeeding generations (Buss, 2015, p. 265).

In other words, as a lone individual one could not survive for long, therefore one's genes preferred that oneself join some community, even if it did not contain one's cousins. So long as one contributed to that community's thriving, the group would reciprocate by offering protection, and the opportunity to mate and procreate.

Most altruistic species are less extreme in their self-sacrifice than ants and termites. They combine altruism with some measure of individual selfishness. Creatures such as wild dogs, dolphins, elephants, and ravens among many others, all risk their individual well-being on occasion in support of others — not robotically, like soldier ants, but through acts of individual choice. On occasion, they also choose not to prioritize the group. This seems to explain why most altruistic species, including the ancestors of modern humans, contain alpha figures. These group leader-rulers allow a good measure of individualism, but also forcefully ensure group loyalty when necessary.

But why individualism at all? Darwin's theory of natural selection rested upon his observation of constant gene mutation resulting from natural causes beyond a creature's control. Most gene mutations were not useful to a species, hence individuals who possessed them fared no better than those who did not -- and sometimes worse. But not infrequently, mother nature brought about environmental changes that most members of a species could not cope with. For instance sudden sustained rainfall to a region of hard-packed soil, where a species of short-legged birds pecked with hard pointed beaks for seeds and tiny worms. Most could no longer gain enough sustenance to survive when the land became swampy. But a few birds with long legs, and broader beaks, who had always found desert survival difficult if not impossible, were now well suited to the new environment. They survived, passed along their mutated genes to their offspring, and kept the species alive. It was it's combination of individualism and altruism that sustained the species. Sometimes a disease arose that killed off all species members save a few possessing life-saving gene mutations. These few were able to rebuild the species. Among humans, sometimes people with skills of negotiation contributed more to group survival than those with skills of warfare. Sometimes the skills of a great tracker of animals, perhaps a young female, was the only band member who could make continued survival possible.

In general, individual diversity, when combined with altruism, enhanced species survival among group animals, more than did the programmed collaboration of virtually identical community members. Which raises the question, how did the authoritarian, or alpha-leader (usually male) management of communities among many mammalian species, including nearly all primates, enhance the beneficial expression of individualism more than allowing them to express their individualism as equals? According to David Buss, though humans practiced reciprocal altruism, they also competed at mate selection, striving to maximize their social status as individuals. To manage the social conflict created by this competition, authoritarian social control might have been essential lest such conflict undermine a band's solidarity, hence weaken its ability at hunting and foraging, as well as at warfare -- no less for humans than for other apes. On the other hand, Buss also expressed awareness that among humans the most important quality of an ideal mate was often not their possession of alpha-quality physical genes. Rather it was their willingness to commit to full partnership, especially in raising offspring. Humans take longer than any other mammal to wean their infants, and family and community support remain crucial throughout teenage and adolescence. Honoring cultural norms regarding mate selection improves community support. All of this suggesting that conscious choice, more than instinct, may have played a great enough role in mate selection, to have rendered alpha male control of how our ancestors went about it unnecessary (Buss, 2015, ch. 4).

The relationship between authoritarian rulership and egalitarianism among our ancestors remains under analysis. Since written records exist no earlier than about six thousand years ago, anthropologists rely heavily upon archaeological evidence to draw conclusions. *In The Dawn of Everything: A New History of Humanity* (2021), David Graeber and David Wengrow drew upon the most up-to-date records to conclude that this relationship was complex. Overall, our ancestors appear to have been more egalitarian before than after the Agricultural Revolution beginning about ten thousand years ago. But evidence exists that the opposite was sometimes true as well. Some successful ancient bands and tribes were probably authoritarian, either all or part of the time. Furthermore, while most ancient humans hunted and foraged in bands of fifteen to thirty people, where egalitarianism would presumably have been easiest to maintain, evidence of egalitarian hunting-foraging communities containing thousands of people. The authors perceived that for about five millennia our species has been stuck in a self-destructive kind of authoritarian form of social organization, which many scholars, along with the public at large, assume was the inevitable consequence of human society becoming massive, urbanized, and complex following the Agricultural Revolution. Graeber and Wengrow find no evidence in support of this assumption, and considerable evidence in contradiction of it. (pp. 423-524).

In *Motivation and Personality* (1943), psychologist Abraham Maslow proposed a hierarchy of human needs that has been studied and discussed in thousands of psychology and sociology college and university classes ever since. First, come basic physiological needs, then the need for safety, then for belonging, then for esteem, and at the top of the pyramid, the need for self-actualization. Nowhere did Maslow assert that any of these needs implied people's craving for greater power or privilege than other members of their community. Self-actualization might involve becoming a dominant figure in one's area of expertise, but it might also involve becoming a beloved figure, or an adept collaborator among equals.

Psychologist Dacher Keltner observed, moreover, that healing the wounds inflicted by conflict characterized humans in particular.

...early hominid conflict differed from that of many other species: it was met with evolved capacities to reconcile (Keltner, 2009, p. 65).

E.O. Wilson (1978) labeled what Keltner observed, an instance of selfish-gene manipulation:

...Human beings appear to be sufficiently selfish and calculating to be capable of indefinitely greater harmony and social homeostasis [social stability]. *...* The genius of human sociality is in fact the ease with which alliances are formed, broken, and reconstituted... *Human behavior -- like the deepest capacities for emotional response which drive and guide it -- is the circuitous technique by which human genetic material has been and will be kept intact. Morality has no other demonstrable ultimate function* (pp. 153-167).

In other words, altruism serves to strengthen human thriving by making the social contract a harmonious, joyful, voluntary experience. This view of what is often called free will, however, remains controversial. Can selfishness really promote community, or is it always too potentially disruptive to be allowed much free expression? Theoretically, well-controlled selfishness should promote thriving better than utter unselfishness. Ideally, a community that maximizes both self-actualization and group-actualization should adapt more flexibly than a group maximizing only the latter, for reasons already mentioned. However, as Buss and Wilson suggest, unless selfishness could be tempered, such an ideal might be unrealizable. Evidence from psychology and neuroscience asserts that modern humans may well be capable of such self-control.

Part 4: Attachment, Affect Regulation, Empathy, and Compassion

During the 1950s, psychologist John Bowlby observed mothers' and infants' interactions directly, rather than relying upon the reports of adults undergoing psychoanalysis, and concluded that the nature of the parent-child attachment, especially during the first four years of life, constituted the most important logical focus of psychology. Thus began Attachment Theory, which has become perhaps the strongest driving force of modern psychotherapy. Together with Mary Ainsworth, he followed children's development over time, finding evidence that their attachment experience during the first four years of life powerfully shaped how they functioned as socialized adults. Bowlby and Ainsworth (1980) found that an imperfect child-parent attachment experience detracted significantly from one's ability to handle the ordinary stresses of life (see also Schore, 1994; Fonagy, 2002; Goleman,1996 and 2006; and Cozolino, 2006).

A person's ability to control strong emotions triggered by an event causing them to feel angry, sad, or afraid resulted from their having experienced what Bowlby and Ainsworth called a secure attachment experience during childhood. Instead of lashing out, bolting, or sinking into deep depression, one could call upon one's memory and cognitive centers to formulate strategies for dealing with a perceived threat in a strategic, reasoned way. The lengthy time required for development of this skill went far toward explaining why human childhood lasts so much longer than that of other mammals. Primates in general take longer to raise their young, but humans take by far the longest of any primate.

According to attachment theorists, through secure attachment, human children develop what psychologists call empathy. The first component of empathy is a "theory of mind." This means grasping how another both resembles and differs from oneself, especially, concerning how you both feel about something. For example, can you tell whether a joke that amuses you amuses your friend? Can you tell when they are amused if they express it differently than you do? What about sadness, fear and anger? The second component is the ability to "mentalize," meaning holding onto awareness of one's own feelings when experiencing someone else's feelings. "I'm angry at what that person did, but I get that you're not, and it's okay for us to be different." The third component, affect regulation, involves the ability to regulate one's emotions, or affect, in service of engaging with another in a functional way. For example, can you use your words rather than your fists to express anger when someone insults you? Good affect regulation enables the adult a child will become to include a full range of feelings in their engagements with others. One can interact without fear of becoming overcome by urges that interfere with their compassion and their ability to reason. Affect regulation strengthens individuals, and by extension the communities they belong to. Affect-regulated people can form strong bonds and rely upon one another. In *Social Intelligence* (2006), Daniel Goleman reports research finding that *the innate altruistic impulse that follows from empathy with someone in need can become muddled, suppressed, or overridden when people feel the anxiety of insecure attachment...* In a series of experiments, securely attached people were *the most willing among the volunteers to lend a hand. Their compassion appears to be directly proportional to the need they perceive: the greater the pain, the more they help* (pp. 213-215).

Affect regulation and sociality

Psychologist and neuroscientist Louis Cozolino (2006) views affect regulation as a major source of human joy. *Our ability to enjoy being inside of ourselves, successfully engaging with others, and managing life's day-to-day stressors depends on the attainment of affect regulation...[involving] the inhibition of impulses and emotions while maintaining a memory for future consequences. In addition, these actions require that we keep long-term goals in mind, flexibly solve problems, and consider the perspectives and needs of others. ... In one sense, a child 'borrows' the prefrontal cortex of the parent while modeling the development of its own nascent brain on what is borrowed...The presence of good-enough caretakers greatly contributes to the development of circuits that are vital to affect regulation and the social brain* (p. 86.)

Over-simply, here is how this works. Soon after emerging from the womb, an infant gazes intently into the eyes of its mother (or other primary caregiver), and they gaze back with equal compulsion. This begins their attachment process, and through it, the infant becomes socialized as a group animal. The drive to attach is genetic and all group animals possess it. Initially, mother is only a source of food and protection, and when an infant is not fed on time or is startled, it screams. As it grows, it gradually shifts from screaming to opening and closing its mouth, or making grabbing motions with its fingers. A little later it begins to shout words like "EAT!!" and "MA-MA!!!" It is thought that all mammals experience this genetically hardwired process, but none with the sophistication of modern humans. During the first four years of life, children progress from "eat!" to "Me hungry!" to "I hate you!" to "I feel really angry at you right now!" when deprived of a sweet before dinner time.

An Infant achieves such self-control in a manner analogous to how a car creates motion. Its brain contains a special, genetically designed system of parts, organized in a particular way; just as a car contains a carburetor and pistons and spark plugs and valves organized in a particular way that we call an engine. We can call the system in the brain, the affect-regulator. The affect-regulator receives information when the infant and mother gaze at one another. The car engine receives gasoline and electricity when the ignition is turned on. Once in operation, the car engine transforms gasoline and electricity into motion. The brain's affect-regulator transforms the information it receives into self-control. The brain accomplishes this feat by creating nerve cells and adding them to the neocortex part of itself. This is the part that prioritizes reasoning in response to perceived threats, rather than automatic, instinctive, acting out. Using the affect-regulator's nerve cells, the brain soothes strong feelings, which can be thought of as alarms set off when more primitive parts of the brain perceive threats to well-being. It does this well enough to allow the infant to choose how to strategize rationally in response to such alarms. To maximize this skill, the child practices expressing strong feelings in words rather than through actions -- repeatedly and continuously, for several years.

When a child affect-regulates well, when she feels anger toward a school friend because he won't share a toy, but also realizes that he might be afraid of losing the toy, she responds to him with empathy rather than rage. However, empathy does not necessarily imply compassion or kindness. Conceivably, one might employ empathy to manipulate another rather than to connect with them in friendship. Such behavior is hardly unknown. The slick salesman sensing a customer's craving for affection can play on that to gain a sale without caring a whit about the customer's welfare. In "Born To Be Good" (2009), Dacher Keltner seeks insight into whether empathy more often implies compassion or opportunism among our species. Well aware that the past five thousand years supply plenty of evidence of opportunistic manipulation, he concludes that compassion is our dominant trait (2009).

Advances in DNA measurement, in archeology, and in the study of our primate relatives are yielding striking

*new insights into the history of humanity… Born To Be
Good reveals how survival of the kindest may be just as
fitting a description of our origins as survival of the fittest.
(p.x) … [T]hose hominid predecessors guided by emotions such as compassion, embarrassment, and awe
fared better in the tasks of survival, reproduction and
raising offspring to the age of viability* (p. 51).

Franz de Waal (2019) documents how compassion also
enhances group thriving among chimpanzees.

*Alpha males are not born, and they don't achieve their
position based purely on size and temperament. The primate alpha male is a much more complex and responsible being than a bully. Merciless tyrants do sometimes
rise to the top in a chimpanzee community, but the more
typical alphas… protect the underdog, keep the peace
and reassure those who are distressed. This male acts
as the healer-in-chief. …* [Moreover] *alpha chimpanzees
are frequently removed from power, and often killed by
band members coalescing in a way that cuts across their
hierarchical ranks, when an alpha's bullying or selfish
behavior becomes excessive* (p. 28 and pp.175-88).

This by no means implies that chimpanzee band members' pursuit of pecking-order status is anything but constant and often deadly. The compassion Dachner Keltner
observes in humans characterizes most primates, but it
finds the most advanced expression in humans. Over
evolutionary time, natural selection seems to have cho-
sen bands that lacked compassion as a defining attribute,
for extinction. Unable to cooperate as effectively as their
compassionate competitors, they became replaced by
them. Bands in which people treated one another the
most kindly, were presumably not only the best strate-
gists at hunting and foraging, and at knowing when to
negotiate and when to fight, they were also the strongest
when it came to inter-band conflict.

If the girl in the above example affect-regulates well, her desire for the toy competes with her desire to stay connected with the boy who owns it, especially if he is a member of her ingroup. Her language skill and empathy enable her to express her feelings in a way that honors both her individualism and her altruism. She still wants to play with the toy, still feels anger at his withholding it, but she pursues her goal in a cooperating rather than a competing way. However, what if the boy is only visiting her school? What if he lives in another city, comes from a family with a different religion than hers, and in other ways exists outside of her ingroup community? Why should compassion play a role in how she deals with him?

In *Psychological Intelligence* (1996), Daniel Goleman titles the section beginning on page 104, "Empathy and Ethics: The Roots of Altruism," wherein he reports the conclusion reached by "empathy researcher Martin Hoffman" indicating that

... the roots of morality are to be found in empathy... [S]tudies in Germany and the United States found that the more empathic people are, the more they favor the moral principle that resources should be allocated according to people's need (pp. 105-6). ... Whenever people come together to collaborate... there is a very real sense in which they have a group IQ, the sum total of the talents and skills of all those involved... The key to a high group IQ is social harmony. It is this ability to harmonize that, all other things being equal, will make one group especially talented, productive, and successful and another -- with members whose talent and skill are equal in other regards -- do poorly.... [T]here is virtually no relationship between being an expert and being seen as someone people can trust with their secrets, doubts, and vulnerabilities (pp. 160-62).

These conclusions reinforce the conclusion reached in part 3: reciprocal altruism greatly enhances the functionality of human society. Affect regulation strengthens altruism by enabling people to prioritize compassion over selfish opportunism. For the girl, simply the fact that the boy was a person would trump all other considerations. Pragmatism alone might conceivably be enough to motivate her to treat him respectfully -- she might need him sometime in the future -- however, her empathy would make it apparent how like her he was, and how she might feel if treated unkindly in similar circumstances. Her ability to self-regulate would allow her to choose to express her innate altruism in a compassionate way, and thereby experience the joy of promoting social harmony.

Conversely, treating the boy incompassionately would deprive her of this joy. It would nullify the harmonious social contract that humans seem instinctively to crave. She would enter into future collaborations assuming that others operated as she did, driven only by selfish pragmatism. This would undermine the functionality of a collaborative community based on mutual trust, caring, and deep connectivity. It would negatively affect her well-being as well as everyone else's. As Goleman suggests, an entire community composed of people operating incompassionately toward others might well be characterized as socially pathological -- as ill. This hypothesis awaits empirical testing, however. The damaging effects of a flawed attachment process (ideally, a kind of harmonious social contract) upon individuals, is now well established, but this is not yet the case as concerns how communal incompassion negatively affects group adaptivity.

Studies of Post Traumatic Stress Syndrome, and similar conditions, indicate that even when the attachment experience during early childhood was secure if a person suffered trauma of certain kinds, affect regulation could be undermined. Any child, teenager, or even adult systematically subjected to physical abuse or shaming, or denied the opportunity to self-actualize in other ways, might find themselves unable to self-regulate well enough to engage well in trust-based collaboration with others (Cozolino, 2006, Part V). On the other hand, research also confirms that the harmonious social contract highlighted by E.O. Wilson appears not just to produce joy, but to produce healing. Modern attachment-based psychotherapy has made remarkable gains over the last several decades in helping people to accomplish such healing, by creating just such a contractual relationship as a central element of treatment (Cozolino, 2006, Part VI).

Perhaps such an approach will eventually find application on a social scale. People joylessly bonded by hatred of others, rather than by compassion, instead of being maligned as racist or sexist or stupid or mean, might be invited to engage with healthier people ready to embrace them should they accept the invitation to heal.

Summing up

Evolution, whatever else it accomplishes, tends to maximize the thriving of life. For animals at least, and growing evidence suggests perhaps for plants as well, this means the maximization of competent, social collaboration. The individual in the group thrives better than the individual alone. A primitive form of communal collaboration characterized some of the very first organisms to inhabit the planet. These were prokaryotic bacteria -- single-celled organisms lacking even a cell nucleus, much less any kind of brain. These organisms still exist, virtually unchanged, and can be studied in modern laboratories. Their life consists mainly of floating independently of one another in a kind of organic soup. However, as the result of no identifiable forces operating on them, now and then these *prokaryotic bacteria choose to form stable groups shielded by protective membranes and crusts, structures called biofilms (Wilson, 2019, p. 69).*

This communal configuration seems to render them less vulnerable to destruction by other organisms.

With the evolution of complex, eukaryotic cells, which contained a nucleus, or command center, organization improved. The nucleus directed various cell bodies, with specialized functions, at accomplishing tasks essential for thriving. Thus the cell itself constituted a tiny society. The leap from this simple organic community, managed by a single dominant individual, the cell nucleus -- such as an amoeba; to a complex organic community involving multiple cells, managed by a brain -- such as a wolf; to a social community of diverse multicellular organisms, managed by an alpha figure -- such as a wolf pack; was only predictable from an evolutionary point of view (Wilson, 1975). Sooner or later, if this has not already occurred, the vector of evolution seems bound to produce a large-brained creature capable of sophisticated, egalitarian group collaboration. A community of highly bonded, highly communicative individuals, self-controlling enough to maximize both altruism and free will, drawing upon the diverse skills of its entire membership rather than solely upon an alpha leader, would maximize rational social decision making. Evidence that this evolutionary step characterized our ancient ancestors grows, but remains inadequate to convince some scholars.

The alpha-male-dominated communities of the apes who gave rise to modern humans elevated the status of males over females. Cave art dating back twelve thousand years or more suggests that among modern humans, however, females played as prominent a role as men in the design of society (Eisler, 1988, ch.2 & Welker, 2017). *Both women and men would make key decisions, such as when to move camp or whether to leave one band and join another* (Harman, 1979, pp. 3-8).

Anthropological studies describe such egalitarian collaboration among some existing cultures that retain strong connections to their ancient roots, but these are very small communities and not representative of modern industrial society. No one can deny that for at least the last five to seven thousand years human society has been predominantly authoritarian. Parts 5-8 explore why and how this developed, and part 13 directly challenges the argument that in modern complex society, without the authoritarian control of alpha leadership, human beings are incapable of much functional cooperation. Two particular sources of evidence are offered now, however, suggesting that when authoritarian control is relaxed, egalitarianism produces better results even in modern society.

During the 1960s, a major concern of industry was how to maximize imagination and innovation toward creating more competitive products, or better marketing techniques, or simply better products and services. Typically, the leadership of a team assigned to carry out such a project was selected by management. Project teams were expected to operate in a fairly authoritarian manner. A mass of small group studies heavily motivated by the work of psychologist Kurt Lewin, found, however, that when project team members were allowed to select their own leadership, and define their own decision-making process, far better results emerged. This came to be labeled laissez-faire management. On the other hand, If a project involved carrying out routine tasks, essentially just following a recipe, authoritarian management usually produced satisfactory results more quickly (Hare,1976, ch. 13). These findings fundamentally transformed corporate management in the United States and spread globally. Corporations and other institutions did not become less fundamentally authoritarian, but they did include egalitarianism on a limited scale and in a controlled way -- with remarkable results. Efforts to expand the inclusion of egalitarianism within a corporate framework continue to find modest support (Seppala and Cameron, 2015). No

studies indicate that egalitarianism weakens rational corporate decision-making.
.
In his 2004 study, *The Wisdom of Crowds,* James Surowiecki described how minimizing authoritarian controls
maximized another kind of group wisdom. Groups of
strangers were asked to estimate such things as the
number of marbles in a jar, a meaningless puzzle; or the
likeliest place to find missing submarines based upon
some written descriptive material, a critical issue. The
defining conditions of the exercises were that subjects'
estimates could be quantitatively averaged and that subjects could not influence one another or be under the influence of anyone else. The experiment was repeated
many times using different setups and involving both
moderate and large numbers of subjects. It turned out
that none of the individual subjects' estimates ever came
very close to the mark. However, the average of their estimates was invariably a near bullseye. Although no altruistic collaboration was involved in these exercises,
Surowiecki's findings contradict the hypothesis that authoritarian control enhances communal rationality. Efforts
to explain Surowiecki's findings are ongoing, especially
within the business community.

Section II: When Everything Changed

Part 5: The Agricultural Revolution

As noted in part 3, until about twelve thousand years ago, archaeologists tell us that our Eur-Asian ancestors' for the most part lived in small hunting-foraging bands, each roaming its territory, carefully avoiding unnecessary conflict with other bands, knowledgeable of the migration patterns of the animals and the growing cycles of the many edible plants occupying their niche. Then, suddenly, many settled into villages, including perhaps a dozen or so bands, and also tribes consisting of two or three bands melded together. They had given up hunting foraging to become horticulturalists, cultivating and consuming mainly grains such as wheat, corn, oats, rice, sorghum, buckwheat, and barley. This diet provided only a fraction of the nutrition of a hunter-forager diet, which in addition to grains and grasses included tubers, fruits, nuts, seeds, meat, and fish. A smaller number of people turned to pastoralism, a nomadic lifestyle that involved domesticating animals, for use as both labor and food. Horses, camels, donkeys, and cattle hauled and carried materials, supplies, and people, pulled plows, extracted stumps, and moved boulders from fields to be sewn with grain seeds by horticulturalists, with whom pastoralists traded and for whom they sometimes worked in exchange for food and occasional lodging. Dogs served as companions, hunters, and guarders. Pastoralist nomadism was necessary in order to provide fresh grazing land for their animals. These dramatic changes in thriving strategy became known as The Agricultural Revolution, which anthropologists also called the Neolithic Revolution because of the dramatic increase in the variety and use of stone tools by our ancestors.

Archaeologists surmise that the Agricultural revolution first occurred in the Fertile Crescent, an area today comprising parts of Iraq, Israel, Syria, Lebanon, Egypt and Jordan. During the following centuries, it both spread from its origins and arose spontaneously in every corner of the planet, far from its origins.

We have clear signs of relatively independent agricultural origins in western Asia, central China, the New Guinea highlands, Mesoamerica, the central Andes, the Mississippi basin, and possibly western Africa and southern India. These developments occurred at many different times between about 12000 and 4000 years ago. The agricultural systems concerned spread at remarkably different rates — some quickly, some slowly, some hardly at all (Bellwood, 2005, p. 3).

Until the mid-1960s, anthropologists confirmed Charles Darwin's description of the Agricultural Revolution in Eur-Asia as a significant advance in human civilization. Nowadays, most view it differently. If it set in motion the forces that produced the modern technologies of today, it did so at a heavy cost that only now becomes fully understood. In *The First Farmers: the origins of agricultural societies,* Peter Bellwood observed that *Hunter-gatherers ... lifestyle, in terms of long-term stability and reliability, has been the most successful in human history* (2005, p. 2).

Modern humans had long known about farming, but until about ten millennia ago practiced it rarely because hunting and foraging provided a healthier diet and was less labor-intensive. He perceived two main forces to be responsible for their dramatic change of behavior. Especially in the Fertile Crescent area of the Middle East, climatic conditions unfavorable to hunting and foraging may have lasted much longer than usual about ten thousand years ago. It was not unusual for hunter foragers to turn temporarily to farming, but this time perhaps the conditions requiring it lasted so long that sedentism became permanent. However, a far likelier explanation was the steady expansion of the human population of the planet (Bellwood, 2005, ch. 2).

From cave art, and other evidence, archaeologists infer that hunter-forager bands were usually egalitarian. They strove knowledgeably and with foresight to respect the ecological niches they occupied. They could elaborately describe the animals and plants they relied upon, and make inferences about their behaviors. Too large a band harvesting food would destroy a niche, and so bands controlled their size in two ways: by reducing birth rates when necessary, and by dividing -- one band remained in the current niche, and the other found a new one. (Graeber, 2021, pp. 92-102; Wilson, 1998, pp. 226-9; Hammond, 1971, pp. 300-302). At a certain point, however, so many bands occupied an area that all available niches were taken, and warfare became likely unless nomadism was abandoned. Modern humans were too equally matched for warfare to become a productive option, and so sedentism became permanent, for most. However, as noted in part 3, evidence exists of some very large communities consisting of many hunter-forager bands, that somehow avoided either authoritarian rulership or warfare (Graeber, 2021). As noted, a few turned to pastoralism, thus continuing to live as nomads. In the final analysis, overpopulation of the species seems to have been a consequence of band splitting beyond the ability of otherwise rational people to foresee (Harari, 2015, pp. 48-49, p. 84).

In *A People's History of the World: From the stone age to the new millennium* (2008), historian Chris Harman described how because it was so labor-intensive, farming for any length of time furthered population expansion to the point where conflict could not be avoided. To eke out a living, bands had to bear more offspring than when they hunted and foraged. The more villagers that needed to be fed, the more land must be taken over and cleared, and the less range became available for pastoralists. This became a source of friction between villagers and pastoralists, some of whom began to raid villages for food and other supplies. They also warred with one another over grazing areas (Harari, 2015, pp. 10-17; Harman, 15).

Yuval Harari reinforced Bellwood's and Harman's observations. Concerning the common perception of the agricultural revolution as a significant advancement of human society, he responded:

That tale is a fantasy. There is no evidence that people became more intelligent with time. Foragers knew the secrets of nature long before the Agricultural Revolution, since their survival depended on an intimate knowledge of the animals they hunted and the plants they gathered. Rather than heralding a new era of easy living, the Agricultural Revolution left farmers with lives generally more difficult and less satisfying than those of foragers. Hunter-gatherers spent their time in more stimulating and varied ways, and were less in danger of starvation and disease. The Agricultural Revolution certainly enlarged the sum total of food at the disposal of humankind, but the extra food did not translate into a better diet or more leisure. Rather, it translated into population explosions and pampered elites. The average farmer worked harder than the average forager, and got a worse diet in return. The Agricultural Revolution was history's biggest fraud (p. 79).

Part 6: The Division of Labor in Society 1: Urbanization

Wherever people adopted agriculture, population exploded. Villages of a hundred or more people grew more numerous in a region and began to crowd one another. At a certain point, villages combined and cities numbering in the thousands of people arose on the planet. Around five or six thousand BCE, pastoralist bands living in areas where farming was difficult, such as the Asian Steppes (a narrow strip of semi-arable land including parts of northern China and southern Russia, extending from Bulgaria in the West to Manchuria in the East), joined forces, armed themselves with arrows and spears with strong, sharp flint tips (and later bronze tips), climbed upon the backs of their recently domesticated horses, and rode long distances to raid and often pillage these early cities. Two thousand years later they were joined by camel riders from the Middle Eastern deserts (Sjoberg, 1960, part II; Harman, 2008, pp. 45-87).

The class division of society

Cities responded to raiders' attacks by building armies of defense, which they also used to conquer rural villages in their hinterlands. At a certain point, any resemblance between the social organization of cities and that of horticultural villages, much less hunter-forager society, disappeared. For the first time in history, modern human communities looked like what Thomas Hobbes described in his famous 1651 treatise, *Leviathan*, as the ideal construction of human society: a mass of citizens controlled by one or a few strong authoritarian leaders. Here is how this came about.

Farming in horticultural villages around 7000 BCE required more than just crop cultivation. People had to clear forests, drain marshes, trench and repair irrigation channels, construct dams, dig wells, make plows and other equipment, collect dung for fertilizer, terrace hill-sides, construct fences and wagons, and create a military force. Some tasks involved an entire village but others were specialized. Among hunters and foragers, a little task differentiation -- what sociologists call division of labor -- had always existed, such as between younger and older people, and between adults and children; and some individuals had always been viewed as experts in one area or another. But for the most part, the entire adult community collaborated to deal with threats and challenges, and in general to achieve common goals. Now things were different. Many tasks became specialized. People who engaged in these tasks often came from different bands and tribes, and they formed bonds independent of those loyalties.

As a result of this complexity, one specialized task emerged that did not involve physical labor of any kind. It was the coordination of all of the other tasks. This fell to a group similar to today's town council, led by a person similar to today's mayor, called Big Man, or Chief. This labeling is based on anthropological studies of modern communities possibly resembling our early neolithic forbears, however, no evidence supports the assertion that this role was necessarily gender-specific, and a good deal of indirect evidence suggests that it very possibly was not. Therefore, the gender-neutral term chief will be used in this essay. Together with a cohort of friends, usually some of their clan members, a chief facilitated and administrated the division of labor. Some surely possessed special prestige and honor, but archaeological evidence indicates that they did not usually possess unique rights and privileges. Chiefs participated in defining village policies, but it was bands and tribes that authorized and endorsed their actions (Harman, 2008, pp. 3-32).

When large cities emerged, first in Mesopotamia, then in Western Europe, North Africa, China, and Central Africa, task coordination became a much greater challenge. The crop-growing acreage of a city dwarfed that of a village, but the number of people per acre grew as well, and so farming continued to demand a large labor force. Not so much, however, as to require everyone in the city to engage in it. Traders, artisans, craftsmen, teachers, doctors, entertainers, bakers, and others, offered goods and services for practical application, but also for pleasure. Agricultural surpluses produced wealth that people individually, and the community at large could use to purchase these offerings. Some of it could be stored as savings, with which merchants could purchase from traders such things as agricultural equipment, or building materials, or weapons, or spices, or garments not available locally, but produced in other cities. To take charge of and manage these surpluses, as well as to take on the heavier demands of coordinating the expanded division of labor, city chiefs required more authority than chiefs had needed to coordinate village affairs.

Coordination quickly expanded into full-fledged management. Chiefs were called upon to plan and administer social policies effectively and efficiently with less and less involvement or oversight by tribal representatives. Chiefs gained enough control over agricultural surpluses to allow them to exploit these for personal gain. They could, if they wished, become not just highly respected figures, but wealthy, powerful manipulators. Archaeological findings based on cave art, burial sites, and the layout of villages, towns, and cities, indicate that this failed to occur for about the first two thousand years of urban life. Egalitarianism remained a strong cultural value (Graeber, 2021, pp. 443-492, 517-18; Harman, 2008, pp. 3-16; Welker, 2017).

And then it did not. Beginning around five thousand years ago, chiefs, now exclusively men, became rulers. In *The Pre Industrial City* (1960), sociologist Gideon Sjoberg described how urbanites were not just differenti-

ated according to the jobs they performed, they also became divided into social classes. A small upper class
consisted not of chiefs any longer, but of monarchs, and
their cohorts. These included high priests, military com-
manders, landlords, barons, wealthy merchants, chief
educators, and the top bureaucrats of city management.
This class established autocratic control over city planning and policy, imposing rules and regulations with
harsh punishments for failure to comply. These could
include horrific measures, such as solitary confinement
and torture, always applied only to the lower class of society, the non-elite inhabitants of the city (pp. 25-51 &
Harman, pp. 22-31).

The lower class was not monolithic, however. Master
artisans and craftsmen, small merchants, some scribes,
skilled workers, small shopkeepers, and soldiers ranked
above less skilled artisans and craftsmen, messengers,
servants, animal drivers, simple farmers, and haulers,
and ditch diggers. These, in turn, ranked above peasants, vassals, slaves, and outcasts. For all its oppressive
nature, this authoritarian social structure created new
opportunities for many people. It freed them from tribal
roles and obligations. They could seek new occupations
and relationships without fear of reprisals that in the past
might have undermined their ability to gain sustenance.
With advances in technology, commerce, travel, explora-
tion, knowledge, and communication, opportunities for
individuals expanded. Some artisans and craftsmen
could live better than others in their tribe, and in general
people could prioritize individualism to a degree never
before possible -- within limits. They were still subordi-
nate to the elite, and subject to the whims of its policies.
The elite made up five to ten percent of the urban population, and dwelled separately from the masses. They
lived opulently, possessed the largest and most richly
appointed homes, and wore the finest clothing. They ate
plenty of meats, nuts, and fruits and received the best
medical care. Much of the lower class lived in hovels,

wore often ragged clothing, lacked clean water, ate only grain-based food, were frequently ill as a result, and rarely received medical care. Between these extremes, a few members of the lower class lived fairly well all of the time, a moderate number fairly well part of the time, and a larger number fairly well only a fraction of the time (Sjoberg,1960, pp.108-44).

Urban authoritarian rulership could vary from city to city in its intensity, and in a single city over time. If from time to time it waned, however, for about the last six millennia it always returned (Graeber, 2021, 443-492).

<u>Warfare becomes normal</u>

For most of the hundred and fifty-thousand years before the social class division of society, warfare had occurred rarely among modern humans. Now it became routine. Nomadic pastoralists eliminated the few hunter-forager bands that occasionally crossed their paths, and pastoralists often fought with one another for control of territory. Cities warred upon pastoralists who roamed across their farmlands, and pastoralists retaliated by raiding them. Cities warred with one another, some successfully enough to grow into city-states, and some of these into empires (the focus of part 8). At the same time, another kind of warfare grew increasingly mature. This was a war upon nature. The agricultural revolution involved the sacrifice of wildlife, both animal and plant, in service of farming and pastoralism. Only species of service to humans were protected and nurtured. Others were either directly eliminated, carelessly but unintentionally destroyed, or left to fend for themselves without access to the ecological niches they depended upon. Urbanism vastly expanded this process. Rather than adapting to natural conditions, humans now strove to manipulate nature with regard only for consequences that enhanced their own immediate comforts. In a few thousand years, the Industrial Revolution would powerfully advance this process.

Part 7: The Division of Labor in Society II: Organic versus Mechanical Solidarity

Scholars who agree with Thomas Hobbes that authoritarian rule is essential to human social organization, often stress the great technological advances of elite-managed modern society, and their benefits to humankind. Though aware that hunter-forager bands may have dealt with environmental and ecological realities more rationally than modern societies have tended to do, they view this as a temporary condition. It results from the size and complexity of modern society that elites will soon learn to manage. It does not indicate a flaw in Hobbe's theory. A growing accumulation of evidence, however, challenges the assumption that authoritarian rulership, or elitism, was either necessary, inevitable, or beneficial (Harman, 2008, Graeber, 2021, Lewis-Kraus, 2021).

The record of hundreds of thousands of years of hunter-gatherer society and thousands of years of early agricultural society show that human nature does not automatically lead to such behavior (Harman, 2008, p.24).

[All] *the evidence we have suggests that, though people surely enjoyed occasional luxuries, most of the time, most of them lived close to subsistence level throughout the agrarian era* (Christian, 2018, p. 234).

The emergence of elitism

In Consilience (1998), E.O. Wilson described how natural selection did not operate so much biologically for our species, as culturally. Research in epigenetics suggested that the genes involved in driving people to create society might not specify how this should be done. They might allow for either authoritarian leadership (or simply elitism) or egalitarianism. At a certain point, culture became the determinant of which approach prevailed among a community. Community's that got it right pre-

vailed. For our most ancient ancestors, this seems to
have meant, for the most part, cultures that preferred
egalitarianism. Usually, elitist cultures probably could not
compete with them. In the modern age, however, human
societies seemed to Wilson so intermeshed that cultural
evolution involved the entire planet. This meant that in
about two hundred years unless humans managed their
relationship with nature better, our species (and most
others) would virtually disappear for anywhere between
several hundred to many thousand millennia. However,
Wilson, and others following him, expressed confidence
that the transformation of society required to avoid such
a consequence, was an altogether achievable goal if
powerful elite policymakers would accept the need for it,
which seemed to him unlikely at present. Failing this,
they must somehow be replaced by people with greater
competence (Ch. 7; Jahren, 2020; Attenborough, 2020).

Based on what has already been presented, it seems not
unlikely that certain stressors arose that could have led
people to embrace elitism as a temporary solution to urban dilemmas, particularly if neither they nor their forbears had ever lived under a monarchy. What if
cultivated grains had been less unhealthy as a staple diet, and what if the iron age and the domestication of
horses and camels had occurred a few hundred years
later? The severity and simultaneity of illness and constant warfare surely weakened the ability of tribal communities to play a dynamic role in city management, and
at the same time made it necessary for chiefs to implement social policies that many citizens found unpalat-
able. As the support and wisdom of tribal councils
diminished, chiefs may have grown frustrated as citizens
criticized and challenged them constantly to "get things
done!" and "find someone else to fight the raiders!" Archaeological evidence reveals that criminality increased
greatly in early cities. Large gangs, called guilds, became prominent and destructive, and the control of guild

behavior fell most heavily upon chiefs and their police forces (Sjoberg, 1960, chs. VII and VIII).

As already noted, archaeological evidence indicates that for at least two thousand years most urban chiefs had no desire to become monarchs. Why this changed remains a question for scholars. The common response that power is seductive, that this is just human nature, fails to satisfy. Long before they became monarchs, chiefs possessed the ability to do so. Did circumstances cause them to gain Hobbesian wisdom, to realize that their citizens needed them to take full and firm control of society? Then why, as we shall see in what follows, did they do this with such frequent cruelty, with such disrespect for their masses, with such ineptitude?

<u>Organic versus mechanical solidarity</u>

The first modern scholarly formulation of the idea that human society best operated as an expression of the will of the people, was, ironically, Thomas Hobbes. No one understood better than the people themselves that creating social stability required a powerful authoritarian hand. They not only accepted authoritarian governance but embraced it. As noted above, Hobbe's ideas gained prominence during the mid-1600s. This was near the end of the renaissance, a period of active philosophical discourse which overlapped the scientific revolution pioneered by Nicolas Copernicus in 1543, ending with Isaac Newton in 1687. Hobbes was called the father of democracy for rejecting autocracy that sought only to maximize the well-being of a ruling class rather than to actualize the will of all the people. John Locke, publishing a few years later, agreed that governance was needed to ensure and protect democracy, however harsh rulership was not. People needed guidance, preferably from those who possessed the intelligence, imagination, skill, and determination to acquire property- -but no citizens required oppression. Those providing guidance should op-

erate in a democratic fashion, none of them seeking to
rule their fellow citizens. During the mid-1700s, the renaissance segued into what was called the enlightenment period of thinking and discourse. It heavily still
featured philosophers, but included more scientists and
mathematicians than before, and witnessed the beginnings of a science of society. In 1762, Jean Jacques
Rousseau supported Locke, and characterized the ruling
classes of modern society as a curse to mankind, virtually enslaving people rather than managing democracy
--not at all the kind of rulers that Hobbes envisioned.
During the early 1800s, Georg Wilhelm Hegel asserted
that human society was ideally democratic, requiring no
elite guidance at all. Sadly, this goal was probably un-
achievable. People should never relinquish democracy
as an ideal, he asserted, but realistically strive to bring
about as enlightened a ruling state as could be achieved.
In 1867, his student Karl Marx, arguing as an economist
and political scientist as well as philosopher, disagreed
with his mentor. Marx perceived that people were more
than capable of achieving full democracy and must aggressively seek to do so, through violent revolution if
necessary. He actively sought to bring such development
to pass. In 1830, French philosopher Auguste Comte
had established sociology as a science, tasked not just
with theorizing, but with empirically testing hypotheses.
His view of human nature fell between Hobbe's and
Locke's: some degree of democracy was desirable, but
this was only achievable through the elite management
of society. Such elites ideally, should heavily include
scholars like himself. In 1893, Emile Durkheim, a founding father of sociology, identified with Comte's view of
an ideal social structure, and the need for elitism, but
also perceived that people's capacity for egalitarian collaboration was substantial. He formulated a theory of social change based on the premise that it constituted the
driving force of social thriving. While autocratic interference with egalitarianism could doom society, he disagreed with Marx that managerial elites could play no

useful role, and must therefore be annihilated. He was the first to give a name to peoples' ability to embrace and utilize reciprocal altruism, without the need for the harsh controls of a Hobbsian leviathan figure. He termed this skill, organic solidarity (Palmer, 1971, pp. 53-69, 296-364; Coser, 1977, p.143; Durkheim,1948, pp.173ff).

In his seminal study, *The Division of Labor In Society,* first published in 1893, Durkheim echoed Marx, proposing that any social organization that blocked citizens' involvement in collaborative policy-making, and failed to maximize the reciprocal altruism of all of its individuals, threatened humanity's very thriving. Such organization created what he called *mechanical solidarity,* where people carried out the will of rulers not as freely choosing individuals, but as obedient servants. What he called *organic solidarity,* on the other hand, allowed people to serve their community as agents of free will, eager to contribute their special talents to enhance its efficiency. They would have no difficulty in accepting the leadership of others whose talents, on occasion, addressed a goal or challenge more saliently than did their own. Durkheim did not, however, advocate revolution to remove barriers to organic solidarity (Durkheim, 1948, pp. xxxi-xxxix).

Durkheim erroneously, as it turned out, rejected the idea that ancient humans might have modeled his theory. He assumed hunter-forager society to be heavily bound by rules and traditions, and band members to have sacrificed themselves to tribal demands, much like worker ants or termites. The advanced division of labor in modern society created the conditions under which people could become free of such obeisance. He proposed that workers should organize into what he called *corporations,* (a very different kind of institution than the term implies today) and consciously achieve organic solidarity among themselves. In agreement with Locke and Hegel, rather than with Marx, Durkheim thought that the property-owning elites of society could accept this development, and invite workers to build society in partnership with them. He died before completing his effort to find evidence in support of his theory and not happily, having acquired considerable evidence that contradicted it. Despite Durkheim's errors and conservatism, his understanding of organic solidarity as not only beneficial to human society, but necessary for its thriving, is considered by many, including this writer, to be one of the most powerful products of social science. It constitutes the driving assumption of this essay (Durkheim, 1948, ix-xxiv).

Rulers' reaction to organic solidarity

Merlin Stone in *When God Was a Woman* (1976), and Riane Eisler, in *The Chalice and the Blade* (1988), presented evidence of how post-agricultural revolution elites always feared the influence of women upon social structure and organization. Rulers assumed that their subjects' urge for equality, and their ability to pursue it had always existed. It had never been destroyed by tyrants, only manipulated and oppressed. They also grasped women's special role for more than a hundred millennia as contextualizers and nurturers of organic solidarity. Women provided its core strength and therefore had to be undermined. Studies of neolithic artifacts show that from 3000 to 1300 BC in Egypt, the depiction of female deities waned from prominent to virtually non-existent, while depictions of male deities increased, along with authoritarian rule and the promotion of mechanical solidarity. Where goddesses represented living in nature and actualizing the human community, gods represented dominating nature and bowing down to rulers.

One of the most controversial issues seems to have been the concept of divine rights to royal privilege, and the institution of hereditary kingship. The earliest laws and myths suggest that the people of the Goddess religion were communally oriented (Eisler, p.128).

Under elite auspices, male dominance and female submission became cultural norms. Communalism, altruism,
and kindness came to be seen as weaknesses. Feminism became distorted to mean caregiving and passive
acquiescence. Women's participation in decision-making
about finances, even at the primary family level, virtually
disappeared. Religion now reified obedience to gods and
carried over to the elite figures who represented them.
Once equal partners with men, women now found themselves subordinated to men, and dependent upon them
for sustenance.

*So universal did it become that even today it is usually
treated as an invariant product of human nature* (Harman, 2008, p. 29).

Graeber and Wengrow (2021) concluded that the deni-
gration of women and the rise of autocracy were so powerfully correlated as to constitute a probably causal
relationship (pp. 433-40, 493-524).

Another strategy undermining organic solidarity was rulers' practice of dividing the lower class of urban society
into sub-divisions, each experiencing a different level of
reward and good treatment. A master craftsman and an
unskilled worker possessed the same status within their
tribe or kinship group, but different statuses as urban citizens. To undermine kinship and tribal ties, citizens received promises of upward social mobility when they
prioritized elite norms (Sjoberg, 1960, pp.138ff).

in his treatise, *The Prince* (1513), Niccolo Machiavelli's
famous advice to monarchs concerning how to maximize
and stabilize their control of the masses, included keeping commoners fairly well satisfied. However, they should
be more afraid than adoring of royalty, and divided in
such a fashion as to minimize ancient connections.
Though he viewed commoners as brutish, Machiavelli
also perceived that they possessed the capacity to make

common-cause, spontaneously and collaboratively. Thus, organic solidarity always posed a threat, emanating not so much from particular individuals, as from the collective (pp. 56-67).

According to Hannah Arendt, in her 1973 masterpiece, *Origins of Totalitarianism*, Adolf Hitler and Joseph Stalin, arguably the two most infamous dictators in history, viewed the masses of their citizens just as Machiavelli suggested. Each went so far as to undermine and destroy the very grassroots movements that brought them to power, out of fear that those who had elevated them could also bring them down. In his 1932 essay, *The Rise and Fall of Elites*, Italian economist Vilfredo Pareto asserted that every ruling class eventually declines due to its fear of organic solidarity. Rulers could not allow the blossoming of innovation essential to the progress of society when it emanated from the lower classes of society -- which was almost invariably the case. Common people must never be allowed to view themselves as participants in social development. German sociologist Max Weber, another founder of academic sociology, reinforced this insight.

[Elite controlled] *Bureaucracy stifled enterprise in Antiquity. There is nothing unusual in this. Every bureaucracy tends to intervene in economic matters with the same result* (Andreski, 1983, p. 365).

There have been many instances of organized response to repression during the last five thousand years, demonstrating to rulers that their fear of the lower classes' ability to draw upon organic solidarity was well-founded. Members of the most oppressed elements of society formed strong solid organizations without the need for authoritarian leadership. Occasionally they achieved remarkable power. For example, the Spartacus movement in 72BCE Rome. When peasant uprisings became too troublesome, the Roman Empire turned to slavery. Slaves hailed from many different cultures, speaking different languages and worshipping different gods. It was easy to keep them disoriented and disconnected, making them far easier to manage than peasants. Nevertheless, a slave named Spartacus organized a rebellion that became strong enough to overthrow the empire. The roman senate expected to be massacred, but this was not the rebels' goal. They sought only to depart Rome and be left alone. The senate gratefully agreed. When it seemed apparent to the Spartacus community that Rome meant what it said, an army was dispatched to stealthily approach and then destroy them.

Why Spartacus threw away the opportunity to try to seize Rome is one of the great mysteries of history (Harman, 2008, p. 80).

In 1795, The Sans-Culottes were citizen-soldiers from the lowest class of French society (sans-culottes meant lacking the fancy trousers of the bourgeoisie) and played a vital role in the revolution's success. However, they received almost none of its rewards and soon found themselves relegated to the status they had previously occupied — virtual slaves to the ruling class. This was no longer French aristocracy, but the revolutionary bourgeoisie, whose mantra had been *Liberté, égalité, fraternité* (liberty, equality, brotherhood). Like the Spartacus movement, the Sans-Culottes organized a force strong enough to unseat their rulers but lacked the sophistication to capitalize upon their achievement. A deal was made, resulting in abject apologies by the bourgeoisie, and promises of fair treatment in the future. Once roiled waters became calm again, forces were dispatched, and the Sans-Culottes massacred (Harman, 2008, pp. 290-302).

In 1920, Mohandas Gandhi asserted that refusing to provide India's British colonial masters with labor, would bring about their withdrawal. A massive movement of powerless citizens embraced his theory, and his leader-

ship. They engaged the British not with violence, but with
what was called passive resistance. This required tremendous courage and strong solidarity on their part.
Thousands were mowed down by machine guns and
killed with other devices as they offered no physical
threat, but only the refusal to work -- interfering with
transportation, farming, and manufacturing by such actions as lying down on railroad tracks and roads, and in
fields waiting to be tilled or threshed, and filling factory
spaces with their bodies. In 1948, Gandhi's prediction
was borne out when the British left India. During the
1960s, Martin Luther King's organization of heavily persecuted black citizens in pursuit of civil rights in the United
States was modeled on Gandhi's movement. It required
and possessed the same solidarity and strength, and had
a substantial impact on social policy (Zinn, 1980, ch. 17).

As we shall see in parts 11 and 12 from 1965 until the
present day, social activism in the United States has consciously embraced organic solidarity as the model for social activism it has grown ever more sophisticated at
defining strategic goals in response to elite failures to
deal functionally with civil rights and environmental concerns (Aronowitz, 1996; Kauffman, 2017; Bond, 2017).

The persistence of mechanical solidarity

Not withstanding the potentialities of organic solidarity,
mechanical solidarity has not been seriously challenged
since it achieved dominance around five thousand years
ago. Some scholars, notably social psychologist Steven
Pinker, argue that this only reinforces Thomas Hobbe's
perception that most people have preferred it and that, for
all of its failures, the alternative would have been far
worse. Followers of August Comte, notably the English
philosopher and sociologist Herbert Spencer, who influ-
enced Emile Durkheim with the argument that the industrial revolution and the rise of capitalism changed
everything, have insisted that elitism is steadily improv-

ing. Karl Marx predicted that when people perceive that mechanical solidarity fails to promote thriving, of any kind, they will reject it. Unfortunately, however, while five thousand years may amount to only an instant of history, they maintain, but it still takes some time to shake off the habits and customs of several millennia. It is not so easy to overcome the inertia of mechanical solidarity and specific strategies must be employed to help this to occur. Members of the anarchist community have disagreed with this assumption. Others, notably social psychiatrist Erich Fromm, fear that living too long in acceptance of authoritarian control may have fatally damaged peoples' innate drive to achieve organic solidarity. Parts 13 and 14 examine these arguments and their implications in detail (Coser, 1977, pp. 3-40, 43-86, 89-125; Fromm, 1970; McClelland, 1979; Fromm, 1970; Pinker, 2011, 2018).

Part 8: The Age of Empires

As noted earlier, the first empire is believed to have been the Akkadian, based in modern-day Turkey about 2300 BCE and lasting until 2154 BCE. In chronological order, here is a list of some of the most studied empires that followed them: The Babylonian empire (1900-1600 BCE), based in modern day Iraq; the Egyptian empire (3000-1077 BCE), based in Egypt; the Kushite, or Nubian empire (760-656 BCE), based in modern day Sudan and Southern Egypt; the Persian empire (550 BCE - 1925 CE), based in modern day Iran; the Macedonian, or Greek empire (334-323 BCE), based in modern day Greece; the Mauryan empire (322-185 BCE), based in India; the Chinese empire (221BCE -1912 CE); the Roman empire (27 BCE-1453 CE), based in modern day Italy and later in Greece; the Arabian empire (622-750 CE), based in the Arabian Peninsula; the Mongol empire (1206-1294 CE), based in Mongolia; the Ottoman empire (1299-1922 CE), based in Turkey; The British empire (1583-1997), based in England. Empires of the Western Hemisphere were the Toltec empire (496-122 CE), based in modern-day Mexico; the Aztec empire (1428-1521 CE), based in modern-day Mexico; and the Inca empire (1438-1533), based in modern-day Peru.

Akkadia

In 2350 BCE, the army of Sargon the Great swept out of the small city of Kish in Northern Mesopotamia to conquer the larger and dominant society of the region, Sumer, in the South. A little north of Kish, near present-day Baghdad, Sargon built Akkad as a base, and then expanded his empire to include all of modern Turkey, Syria, Kuwait, Israel, Jordan, and Palestine. Sargon was a skilled military strategist and warrior, and a harsh tyrant. He treated captives far more ruthlessly than did the Sumerians. He was also an excellent administrator.

Records from Sargon's court show that the empire had a bureaucracy far beyond anything developed to this point in Sumer. Sargon tried to standardize weights and measures within his borders; he also put into place an Egyptian-style tax system, run by state officials who managed the empire's finances (Bauer, 2007, p. 102).

As Sargon aged, however, his administration deteriorated. To support their opulent lifestyle, the ruling class levied crushing taxes upon an already poor peasantry. The rulers who followed Sargon were more oppressive, and their administrations were even more corrupt. Court intrigues became common. About a hundred years after Sargon's demise, in 2154 BCE, his empire degenerated into a kind of unstable feudalism. Small kingdoms fought among themselves while being constantly raided by marauding hordes of nomadic pastoralists. The Achaemenid dynasty of the Persian empire absorbed what was left of Akkadia, in the fourth century BCE (Harman, 2008, p. 33).

Egypt

In 3150 BCE, King Menes united wealthy cities occupying Egypt's Nile Valley into the first of seventeen ruling dynasties. Fifteen hundred years later, Pharaoh Ahmose I, emperor of the eighth dynasty, created The New Kingdom and expanded Egypt to include Nubia (a land located in today's southern Egypt and northern Sudan), and modern-day Syria, Lebanon, Jordan, Israel, and Palestine. Archaeologists have surmised that the New Kingdom did not advance Egyptian society, but diminished it. The highly innovative and productive dynasties of 3000 to 2000 BCE gave way to a stagnant monarchy. Its refusal to modify outdated bureaucratic procedures virtually stifled social progress. The early period had produced advances in irrigation, agricultural technology, medicine, orchard husbandry, fermentation, the production and use of copper, glazing, wheeled vehicles, development of the

arch; and the invention of the sailing boat, the seal, a so-
lar calendar, writing, numerical notation, and the alloy
bronze. During the next two thousand years, only a few
important inventions emerged, and these despite imperial restrictions upon innovation. They were the product of
people on the periphery of Egyptian society, labeled "bar-
barian," and included advances in metal refining, writing,
mathematics, and advanced machineries. Just as occurred in Mesopotamia, the rulers eventually so impoverished the bulk of their citizens that society disintegrated,
and by 1050 BCE its remnants had been swept up by
Persia (Harman, 2008, pp. 32-9).

Greece

During the 500s BCE, the island city-states of Greece
started to use slaves not just as house servants, as was
customary in Mesopotamia and Egypt, but as general
labor.

*Polybus speaks of slaves and cattle as the essential re-
quirements of life* (Harman, 2008, p. 65).

This meant that landowning barons no longer had to rely
on the services of paid peasants, and their wealth greatly
expanded as the large peasant class sunk into poverty.
So also did baron's influence grow, to such a degree that
they were able to eclipse the ancient aristocracy, whose
members had always reined them in. In a state of panic,
a group of these deposed rulers, mainly in Athens, perceived a common interest linking aristocracy and peasantry. Each needed to improve its situation. Aristocrats
called upon peasants to help establish a state of democracy in Greece. This meant that the upper class would
continue to enjoy exclusive ownership of property, including slaves, but peasants would attain some power to protect themselves from the extreme extortions they
suffered at the hands of barons. Even this extremely
narrow concept of democracy impacted Greek culture

profoundly. For two centuries, Grecian thinkers produced a rich body of philosophy and literature that remains in circulation to the present day. In the mid-fourth century BCE, peasants answered Alexander the Great's request for volunteers to build an army capable of creating an empire that would expand Greece to include much of Egypt and the Middle East. Neither Grecian democracy, nor Alexander's reign, however, really changed the relationship between the upper and lower classes. Gradually the former became so self-indulgent and corrupt that the empire declined enough for Rome to absorb it with little effort soon after Alexander's death (Harman 2008, pp. 63-70).

Maurya

In about 1500 BCE, Chandragupta Maurya organized a horde of nomadic pastoralists to conquer and ransack the thriving cities of the Indus civilization of Northern India. Using new iron axes, the farmers they virtually enslaved were able to farm the Ganges jungles well enough to produce agricultural surpluses. These were large enough to produce the wealth needed to build a massive military force, which ultimately gave Maurya control of Northern India; the land trade routes to Iran, Mesopotamia, and the kingdoms of northern China; and the ocean trade routes to Arabia, Egypt, east Africa, and South East Asia. During its early years, the empire advanced because of useful innovations emanating from its lower classes, just as had occurred in Egypt. But by the sixth century BCE imperial excesses and short-sightedness caused Maurya to deteriorate into a state of isolated villages and small kingdoms in perpetual conflict with one another. This lasted for nearly a millennium, a dark age when learning declined and superstition prevailed. In 184 BCE, the Shunga dynasty arose and took control (Harman, 2008, pp. 48-53).

China

Beginning around 2000 BCE in Eastern China, farming settlements along the Yellow and Yangtze rivers combined into cities, and then into city-states, and then into kingdoms. When these were combined, they became the first dynasties of Chinese empire. The first of these, the Zhou, reined from the eleventh to the third century BCE. When rulers refused to adopt new and more efficient methods of farming and farm management invented by the peasantry, while taxing them ever more heavily, the Zhou became easy prey to the Ch'in, who possessed more sophisticated bureaucratic organization and also employed modern military techniques of warfare. When the Chin, in turn, became resistant to innovation, and increasingly oppressive of their labor force, their dynasty fell to the Han. In the early second century BCE, the Han constructed what historians have called a Golden Age in China. It included the invention of paper, the promotion of Confucianism, and the opening of the Silk Road trade routes to Europe. All of this took place under strict imperial oversite, which became increasingly conservative. When the Han discouraged innovations bubbling up from its forward-thinking merchant class, a stagnant kind of stability settled upon Chinese society. Artisans and craftsmen, as well as peasants, lived on the verge of starvation. Magnificent projects such as The Great Walls, the tombs of the emperors, huge palaces, and advanced canals produced only very meager benefits for most citizens. Beginning in the sixteenth century CE, China was taken over by Europeans, who though ignorant and provincial in many respects as compared to the Chinese, were innovative traders and merchants. Many scholars have suggested that had the Han dynasty embraced its merchant class, the world might look very different today (Harman 2008, pp.54-62).

Rome

The Roman Empire began in the sixth century BCE as an Italian village on the Tiber River, that was owned by the Etruscan civilization to the North. By 509 BCE, trade and agriculture had enabled it to become a substantial city, whose management lay in the hand of a group of patrician families. At a certain point, these families declared the city independent of Etruscan rule and declared themselves the Senate of a new republic. Over the next thousand years, this republic, Rome, expanded to include all lands along the Mediterranean Sea, all of Egypt north of Aswan, all of Europe south of the Danube and Rhine River valleys, all of Asia Minor and Syria, and all of Africa north of the Sahara. The wealth required for such military expansion was created by the labor of plebeians, or peasants. Though a heavily exploited class, plebeians were entitled to representation in the Senate. This meant little, however, since they possessed almost no collective political strength. Nevertheless, their potential dissent greatly concerned members of the ruling class, causing it to replace most plebeian labor with that of captured slaves. Slaves possessed no rights, came from diverse cultural backgrounds, and spoke different languages. Unlike plebeians, they seemed to pose no threat of rebellion. By 100 BCE, slaves made up more than forty percent of the Roman labor force (Harman, 2008 pp. 71-86, 117-122).

In time, the dramatic decline of the plebeians, coupled with the voracious greed of the ruling class, created chaotic conditions throughout Roman society. One result of this was the remarkable Spartacus slave revolt described in part 7, another was a relentless succession of plebeian uprisings. In the mid-first century BCE, Julius Caesar, acclaimed Roman general, hero of the Gallic wars, forcibly took charge of things. He disbanded the Senate and installed an era of military rule, only to be assassinated less than three decades later by a member of his ruling clique. Caesar's mantle fell to his nephew Octavian, who received the title Augustus, meaning "The Venerated." As Rome's first emperor, Augustus created an era of peace and prosperity which became known as the Pax Romana. This lasted a little over a century and a half, during which time military expansion continued and the upper class lived better than ever at the expense of the lower classes. For a time, internal conflicts subsided. Eventually, however, the wars of expansion waned, causing the source of slaves, upon which social stability depended, to diminish. Taxes on plebeians increased and finally motivated their return to rebellion. Paying for the military forces required to contain rebellion heavily strained Rome's rulers, just at a time when Germanic tribes based in the Asian Steppes began relentlessly to assault the empire. In response to these pressures, the ruling class left Rome in 330 CE and reestablished a new base in an ancient city in Greece, called Byzantium, which they renamed Constantinople, in honor of the emperor Constantine. The Byzantine empire never achieved the power and domination of Rome, yet lasted nearly three times as long. It fell to the Ottoman Turks during the fifteenth century CE (Harman, 2008 pp. 71-86, 117-122).

The Silk Roads

As travel and communication improved, trade routes opened. Notably the Silk Roads, a system connecting most of Asia south of Russia with Northern Africa and Southern Europe, including the Mediterranean nations. As trade increased, the role of merchants grew. Slaves became an especially valuable commodity, along with silks, spices, textiles, and metals, especially those used for coinage. Early in the thirteenth century CE, the Mongols descended from the Asian steppes along these trade routes, and briefly established, in possibly the most ruthless fashion ever in history, the largest, and ironically, the least oppressive empire the world had known. They were followed by the Ottoman Turks, who brought to an end the empires of Persia and Rome. Gradually, trading and business grew ever more important in establishing the hegemony of empires, at which skills the newest players on the scene, the Europeans, as we shall see in part 9, proved especially adept (pp. 123-135; Frankopan, 2016).

Imperial decline and technological advance

The agriculture-based empires described above, and others like them, differed from one another in many respects, but all had several things in common. Agricultural surpluses provided the wealth that enabled ruling classes to expand militarily. Sometimes they absorbed those they conquered; at other times they plundered them for food, goods, and slaves. Non-elite citizens were rarely included in planning, even when this would have been beneficial to the empire. Imperial decline owed much to rulers' rejection of lower-class inventions and innovations. Nevertheless, during the approximately three-thousand-year period of imperial rise and fall, from around 2000 BCE until about 1000 CE, knowledge grew in all areas. Science and mathematics developed, agricultural technology improved, wealth was more efficiently held in money than in goods, and the seeds of the industrial era to follow were sewn. All of this, however, always to the benefit of ruling classes at the expense of agricultural peasants, finally to such a degree that an empire could no longer be sustained.

Absent imperial fear of embracing the contributions of the entire human community, how much greater might these positive effects have been? Following the French and Industrial Revolutions in Europe during the seventeen and eighteen hundreds, the base of social progress shifted from agriculture to manufacturing on a global scale. With the Industrial Revolution, perhaps authoritarian rulership would improve.

Section III: Modern Society

Part 9: Ascendance of the West

Feudalism in Europe

A new European empire might have replaced Rome. Charlemagne and the Frankish tribes he led during the late 600s CE came close to accomplishing this goal. Instead, Western Europe became divided among warlike, clan-based agricultural estates. This was the era of feudalism in Europe, about which many romantic and adventure novels have been written. Similar systems preceding it in history, usually arising between the decline of one Asian dynasty and the rise of another, were popularized in Europe a millennium later in art and literature about the "exotic East." A European feudal estate contained a substantial, but not palatial, manor that housed a baron, or lord, and his knights, and their families. Acres of fields surrounded the manor, upon which dwelt the peasants who worked the land: serfs. A serf could consider a section of land his to occupy so long as his family worked it diligently and supplied the baron with most of what it produced. Serfs were heavily exploited, but not usually oppressed. Some barons even worked alongside their serfs.

Barons tended to be illiterate, provincial, and crude in comparison with people of their class in the declining Persian and Byzantine empires of Asia. But they were clever innovators. A plow invented by eastern European Slavs during the 6th century AD spread Westward over the next 300 years, increasing the productivity and reducing the labor cost of agriculture to a previously unheard-of degree (Harman, 2008, pp. 140-144).

The rise of monarchs

Conflicts among feudal estates produced coalitions. Some barons were elected by their peers to coordinate a coalition's combined military forces during conflicts with other coalitions. These barons attained the title of King. A king possessed command only over his knights, however. Persuading other barons to instruct their knights to follow his lead in executing military strategies that he had carefully worked out, was often problematic. A way to resolve this frustration arose from the fact that feudal estates employed the services of artisans, craftsmen, and traders living in villages and towns that grew up adjacent to estates. When a king gave them the right to self-governance, they were often ready to provide him with superior tools and weapons, and themselves as paid mercenaries. In this role, they proved quite effective. Barons insufficiently supportive of a king's authority could now be defined as unnecessary, and no longer entitled to his support when they needed it (Harman 2008, pp. 140-168).

Modest kingdoms grew into sizable monarchies centered in large cities, and thence into city-states. The nations of today retain many of their names — Germany, France, Belgium, Spain, Denmark, and England, among others. Constantly at war, and evenly matched, none managed to create a European empire. The competition among them, however, motivated wealthy monarchs to rely more and more heavily upon the assistance of commoners. This resulted in the best weapons, tools, production techniques, and military strategizing the world had yet seen. In *The Age of Revolution: 1789-1848,* (1962) historian Eric Hobsbawm described how the non-elite classes of European society knew very well how much they aided kings to achieve their goals and so pressed for more autonomy in compensation for their services. In England, this gave rise to the movement that produced the Magna Carta, in 1215; the Peasant Revolt (or Wat Tyler's Rebellion), in 1381; and the American Revolution, in 1775. It also produced the French Revolution, in 1789. The Napoleonic wars expanded the French Revolution throughout Europe (and beyond) and thereby weakened feudal aristocracy even more. These developments were both

cause and effect of the Industrial Revolution, which began during the early middle-ages, soon after the fall of
Rome, and came to full bloom in England, in 1760.

The merchant classes of European society soon became
the dominant powers on the planet. They promised the
lowest classes of their societies equality and justice in
return for their support but soon became no less oppressive than their agricultural predecessors. Serfdom ended
in most parts of Europe during the twelfth century, and
during the 1600s many rulers began referring to themselves as constitutional, rather than absolute monarchs.
However, this barely lessened social class inequality. A
series of revolutions in 1848 failed to break the back of
greedy, short-sighted autocracy that rendered the masses of European society impoverished and miserable (ch.
16).

European empires

Beginning in the 1400s, Portugal and Spain, followed by
England, Holland, Belgium, and other European nations
created ocean-going fleets. They soon established trade
with lands in Africa, Asia, and the Americas. A short time
later, they invaded and conquered these vulnerable communities. Their ships were faster, more maneuverable,
and better weaponed than their Asian competitors. In
The Silk Roads (2015), Peter Frankopan described how
European dominance was enhanced by the refusal of
Asian emperors to listen to the advice of their merchants,
traders, and military leaders concerning the rise of the
West. The spread of corruption within the ruling classes
of Byzantium and Czarist Russia, and the advance of the
up-and-coming young Ottoman Empire of Turkey,
drained the military resources of Persia and Constantinople and further contributed to their decline.

In the Western Hemisphere, the situation was different.
Jared Diamond, in *Guns, Germs and Steel* (2005), and

Charles Mann, in *1493* (2011) described how the diseases transmitted by the livestock Europeans brought on their ships was the factor that enabled them to conquer what became the Americas and Canada. In previous centuries, Europeans' own communities had been devastated by these diseases, but the people who survived became immune to them. Western-Hemisphere civilizations could not have escaped annihilation had their invaders been the kindest of planetary neighbors, rather than rapacious conquerors.

Spain and Portugal first, and then Germany, Belgium, Italy, Austro-Hungary, the Netherlands, and Britain sailed out to establish sizable holdings beyond Europe since expansion within Europe was virtually impossible. Peter Frankopan described how between the late 1500s and the early 1900s, through a combination of economic subterfuge, and warfare using advanced weapons, Britain became the most extensive empire the world had ever known. The British subjected all falling under their control to treatments both ruthless and short-sighted, and it was these traits in combination, he concluded, that brought about their decline. Britain so bankrupted those it exploited that they simply dried up as a source of wealth. The result of this decline was armed conflict on an unprecedented scale, producing horrific destruction, a consequence almost certainly avoidable had British policymakers not suffered from the same refusal to acknowledge reality that had infected their imperial predecessors.

[The] mismatch between ambition and ability was a recipe for disaster... Rulership was in the gift of policymakers in London, who had little concern for the interests of local populations (2016, p. 340).

Global warfare

The wealth European monarchies accrued from their colonies financed ongoing conflicts with the Ottoman Empire and Russia, but also among themselves. These expenditures, together with an absence of spending restraint on the part of the wealthy classes, drained European economies. England in particular fell into such debt that only expanded warfare seemed to offer a way out. The result was not one but two world wars. The first lasted from 1914-1918, and the second, a continuation of the first, from 1939-1945. Only slight changes in the constituencies of the warring parties occurred during the interval. The side that triumphed was called The Allies: including England, France, Belgium, Denmark, Russia, and the United States, among others. Those defeated were the Axis powers: including Germany, Italy, Hungary, and also Japan, among others. How much the victors actually won, and how much they lost, has been much debated.

The Great War [World War I] *saw the treasuries of the participants ransacked as they tried to destroy each other, destroying themselves in the process* (Frankopan, 2016, p. 309).

Ultimately, most European empires lost the bulk of their foreign holdings to the wars' victors or to nationalist uprisings in the victors' colonies. England's greatest loss was India, following the brilliant passive-resistance movement led by followers of Mohandas Gandhi, in 1930. However, Britain's global influence began its sharp decline more than a century earlier, in 1783, when its colonies in what became the United States of America gained independence. During the French and Indian War of 1754-63, American colonists had fought alongside British soldiers to douse French aspirations in North America, but Americans' victory in the War of 1812 made it clear that the United States intended to control the Americas without British assistance as well. The Spanish American War of

1898 ended Spanish influence, leaving the United States North America's indisputably dominant power. From the end of the two world wars of 1914-1945, and a subsequent cold war lasting from 1947-1991, until the present day, American hegemony grew to dwarf its parent (Harman, 2008, pp. 543-601; Palmer 1971, pp. 928-995; Hobsbawm, 1987).

The World Wars created horrific devastation, beyond anyone's imaginings, due substantially to the invention of weapons such as the machine gun, and the use of poisonous gasses. Desperate to recruit support from among the lower classes of their societies, European heads of state portrayed themselves as no longer monarchs, but leaders of nations. As nationals, commoners should now view themselves as full-fledged citizens, rather than subjects of royalty. When the wars ended, The United States, the major victorious nation, declared the political ideology of nationalism to be democracy, and its economic policy to be no longer mercantilism, but laissez-faire capitalism. Mercantilism had provided monarchy with tight control over economic profiteering. Under capitalism, profiteering was unconstrained by anything but a lack of imagination, determination, and greed on the part of the new upper class - the businessmen of America (Harman, 2008, pp. 233-57).

Of the three victorious nations that convened in Tehran, Yalta, and Potsdam in 1945 to decide how the spoils of victory should be divided, the United States was the only one never invaded by an enemy during the wars, and one of only two nations to emerge as a true superpower. The other superpower, for a time, was not England, but Russia and a group of satellite republics adjacent to it. Collectively, they were called The Soviet Union.

There was no 'big three' at Yalta, There was a 'big two'
plus one brilliant political entrepreneur who was able to
keep himself and his country in the game, so that Britain

*maintained many elements of great-powerdom well into
the late twentieth century (Zakaria, 2008, p.196).*

To implement the Yalta agreements, a new international
body called The United Nations was created. Ostensibly,
it was to provide a collaborative forum for all of the victorious nations, and others to be included at their discretion.
However, influence was heavily lopsided, and the two
major powers were not friends.

*Although the United Nations Security Council provided
permanent seats for five powers, the war, in effect, left
only two great powers still standing in any strength, the
United States and the Soviet Union....Moreover, the two
were superpowers, continental land giants, possessing
enormous resources and military strength, overshadow-
ing all other states, including the great powers of Europe
that had long dominated events in the modern centuries.... From 1945 on, there set in a diplomatic and ideological clash of interests and ideas which came to be
known as the Cold War, which, with many alterations and
vicissitudes, persisted on into the second half of the
twentieth century* (Palmer, 1971, p. 933).

The East-West Cold War

American democratic capitalism had its strongest roots in
seventeenth-century Holland, but received a kind of for-
mal definition by Adam Smith, in The Wealth of Nations
(1776). Ideally, it meant that only the market forces of
supply and demand would determine economic reality.
An entrepreneur's' pursuit of profit and the public's acceptance of his efforts would be the only factors determining
his success or failure. Coming from a prominent family,
for example, would have nothing to do with it. What Smith
called enlightened self-interest would ensure that while a
businessman might be motivated by greed, he would not
be able to satisfy it unless his offerings conformed with
public norms concerning what was both useful and ap-

propriate. For example, he would not be able to profit from slavery or pornography. Competition for public approval would drive entrepreneurs to constantly innovate, and improve productivity in every imaginable area. In general, entrepreneurs would constitute the wealthier class of society since they created jobs and enhanced national wealth more effectively than anyone else. Politically, democracy meant that the public would elect those whom it wished to govern society. If these men were usually members of the entrepreneurial community, it was because they were the most competent. If men came to occupy the wealthy upper-class of society, this was also because they had earned their status, not because they had inherited it (Heilbroner, 1961, pp. 28-57, 112-142).

In contrast with democratic capitalism, the professed political-economic ideology of the Soviet Union was Marxist communism, an extreme form of socialism. Politically, communism also meant democracy, but a thoroughgoing democracy that involved no social class division of any kind; neither through inheritance nor wealth. Economically, it meant the management of economic challenges through a process of consensual decision making involving all members of society, in some fashion. This was never spelled out in any detail by Karl Marx or his followers. In neither system, should a particular individual or group be allowed to manage political or economic affairs in such manner as to guarantee benefits to themselves and not to others, as had the tzars of Russia and the monarchs of Europe in prior times. As we shall see, neither system practiced what it preached (Heilbroner, 1961, pp. 28-57, 112-142).

What came to be called, simply, The West included the United States and its allies. It was also called the North Atlantic Treaty Organization, or NATO. The East included the Soviet Union and its allies. It was also called The Warsaw Pact. These coalitions did not utilize the United Nations to create global harmony, although millions of their citizens must surely have applauded such an initiative. Instead, they began to jockey for global dominance, initially through economic and political maneuverings rather than through armed conflict. Their inclusion of the general public in working out their goals and procedures was superficial at best (Palmer, 1971, pp. 930-939).

Their commitment to cold rather than hot conflict, however, opened up opportunities for Asian countries previously oppressed and exploited by some of their members.

... it did not take long for leaders in the countries concerned to realize that they could play the two superpowers off against each other — and extract increasingly large benefits from both as a result. Indeed, when President Eisenhower visited Kabul in person at the end of the 1950s, he was asked point-blank to match the aid that was being given to his country by Moscow. Refusal had consequences, but so did acquiescence (Frankopan, 2016, p. 417).

Gradually, negotiation gave way to manipulation as each side attempted to encroach upon the holdings of the other. During the 1950s, this resulted in two brutal conflicts: the Korean War, 1950-'53, and the Vietnam War, 1955-1975. In both cases, these were the result of attempts by the United States to gain influence over Asian lands. Communist China, a rising force within the Soviet Union, played a major role in answering force with force (in 1956 China became strong enough to declare independence of Russia, and become a superpower in its own right). The Soviets found gaining a foothold in the West, especially in Central America and Cuba, to be equally difficult. Compromise, however, was not a consideration for either power (Hobsbawm, 1994, pp. 225-256; La Feber, 1984, pp. 5-14ff).

...It was not long before the combined arsenals of the two superpowers were enough to destroy the world many

times over. Yet generals on both sides played war games which assumed the use of these weapons (Harman, 2008, p. 546).

Finally, in 1962, when Russia seemed poised to establish a military presence in Cuba, the world came to the brink of an all-out war vastly more destructive than anything that had come before. This war would involve nuclear bombs, which had been developed toward the end of WWII and used to obliterate Hiroshima and Nagasaki, two large islands belonging to Japan. Their effects made it clear that warfare involving many of such weapons would not just decimate huge populations, but create a phenomenon called nuclear winter, a term made famous by Jonathan Schell in his book *The Fate of the Earth* (1982). Nuclear winter would create conditions of extreme radiation, and a drastic cooling of the earth resulting from dense clouds of dust blocking sunlight for a very long time. These effects would become so severe as to destroy most of animal life on earth, including humans, possibly for many centuries. Schell's reportage was widely accepted among the global scientific community but seemed to have limited impact upon U.S. or Soviet foreign policy. In neither West nor East did ordinary citizens play a role in deciding their fate.

Transcripts of the US presidential discussions show the government of the world's greatest power was indeed prepared to risk nuclear war with Russia...(Harman, 2008. p. 570).

Russia's prime minister, Nikita Khrushchev, finally agreed to withdraw the missiles, but the prospects of a global disaster did not substantially change the policies of Nato and the Warsaw Pact. They agreed to what was termed detente, a commitment to minimize encroaching upon one another. This did not, however, rule out nuclear aggression as a possible strategy in the future, for either.

Both sides continued to accumulate enormous quantities of nuclear weapons. ...This continued right through to 1980... (p. 570).

Thus, neither superpower operated according to their professed ideologies — which in both cases implied inclusion of the public in the design of social policy, particularly when the thriving of millions was at stake. Each operated little differently than empires of the past, prioritizing the hegemony of their ruling classes over all other considerations, and in a manner that can only be assessed as irrational. In any case, with the cold war's end, which came soon following the Cuban Missile Crisis, the world possessed only one superpower.

By 1991, the bankrupt Eastern bloc collapsed, ending the cold war and leaving the United States of America the leader, and militarily the vastly most powerful member of what was now called Western Empire. Its technological imagination and aggressive creativity, its business acumen, and its educational institutions made it the envy of the world. The industrial revolution, maximized by capitalism, created *more [positive] change to the lives of the great majority of the world's population in the 20th century than in the whole preceding 5,000 years* (Harman, 2008, p. 619).

Part 10: American Democracy Up Close

Challenges confronting the new nation's founding fathers at the constitutional convention convening in Philadelphia during the summer and early fall of 1787, long before it became a superpower, were not much different from those facing industrializing monarchies throughout Europe. Democratization was in the air. The labor needs of manufacturing differed from those of agriculture. Serfs must be retained on feudal estates during a drought because the drought would end and their services would be needed in the future. If a factory failed, on the other hand, workers could, and from a business standpoint, should be laid off. It was more efficient for employers to grant people the freedom to seek employment of their choice, promising them a better shot at a good life for doing so, all the while colluding to control wages and the terms of employment. In this manner, workers' opportunity to market themselves as free men could be advertised as a great benefit of capitalism but undermined in the workplace. As noted earlier, the Greek aristocracy had successfully employed democracy in a similarly deceptive manner.

Nevertheless, the founders of the United States of America worried a good deal that things might get out of hand.

Democratization...raised the most serious problems for those who governed states and for the classes in whose interests they governed... [Specifically,] how to maintain the continuity of sensible policies... (Hobsbawm, 1987, pp. 95-6).

Meaning, how to be sure that citizens would not interpret democracy to imply organizing in defense of their new rights as a working class. In *The American Political Tradition* (1965), Pulitzer Prize winner Richard Hofstadter described the mindset of the men who framed the U.S.

constitution as almost unanimously obsessed with this concern.

Throughout the secret discussions at the Constitutional Convention it was clear that this distrust of man was first and foremost a distrust of the common man and demo-cratic rule. ... [Only] William Few of Georgia... could be said in any sense to represent the yeoman farmer class which constituted the overwhelming majority of the free population (Hofstadter, 1965, pp. 5-7).

How these men truly regarded democracy as an ideal continues to be a subject of debate. Perhaps a substan-tial commitment to democratic principles, as defined by John Locke, did define them. Or perhaps the Founders simply understood that they must protect their position and wealth from one another, as well as from the public.

[George Washington] *repudiated a suggestion that he become a military dictator... remarking that 'we are apt to run from one extreme to the other'* (pp. 7-8).

The debate concerning their genuine motives

...reached a high point in [historian] *Charles A. Beard's An Economic Interpretation of the Constitution of the United States...* [S]*ome readers tend to conclude from his findings that the Fathers were selfish reactionaries...* [Others] *used Beard's facts to praise the Fathers for their opposition to 'democracy'...* (pp. 19-20).

The founders' agreed that so far as participation in poli-cymaking was concerned -- in governance -- democracy should include mainly the wealthiest citizens, and to a limited extent other property owners, but by no means the working class in general. If the Founders could as-suage the anxiety of small property holders, they expect-ed the unpropertied lower class to present little problem.

What encouraged the Fathers ... was the broad dispersion of landed property. The small land-owning farmers had been troublesome in recent years, but there was a general conviction that under a properly made Constitution a modus vivendi could be worked out with them. The possession of moderate plots of property presumably gave them a sufficient stake in society to be safe and responsible citizens under the restraints of balanced government. Influence in government would be proportionate to property: merchants and great landholders would be dominant, but small property-owners would have an independent and far from negligible voice (p.18).

In *Contours of American History* (1961), William Appleman Williams regarded the importance of the debate between James Madison and Alexander Hamilton concerning how to manage the public to be "far from negligible." Hamilton advocated for direct, and when necessary dramatic oppression of public dissent. The upper class should make it crystal clear who was in charge and who was not. Madison argued for an indirect approach: create the illusion of full democracy, and use subtle strategies to structure society so as to ensure that elite control must prevail. This would avoid costly, unnecessary, and potentially elite-damaging conflicts. Madison's arguments prevailed among the founder community. As a result, the emerging U.S. constitution included selection of a president by members of an electoral college, not necessarily precisely reflecting the will of the public; and a legislative body called a senate, where each state, regardless of its population size, would cast the same number of votes for a member of congress. Each of these devices was designed to provide significant leverage on behalf of the wealthiest citizens. Should non-elite property holders become aware of how little power they possessed, they could be offered privileged expansion into new territories.

'Extend the sphere,' he concluded, 'and you take in a greater variety of parties and interests; you make it less probable that a majority of the whole will have a common motive to invade the rights of other citizens; or if such a motive exists, it will be more difficult for all who feel it to discover their own strength, and to act in unison with each other(Williams, 1961, p.161).

All understood Madison's primary goal to be the same as Hamilton's: ensuring the stability of control by the wealthy, and not the promotion of general equality. He is widely regarded as the primary architect of American democracy. Only a few objected to its apparent duplicity.

Luther Martin of Maryland... attacked the Constitution [as]...the work of men who wanted 'one great and extensive empire, calculated to aggrandize and elevate its rulers and chief officers far above the common herd of mankind... (p. 161).

Hamilton never relinquished his opposition to Madison. He predicted that however illusory constitutional freedom was intended to be, non-elite citizens would find ways to use their contractual democracy in ways that none of the founders wished for.

Education for good citizenship

Madison's victory was predictable, according to Antonio Gramsci, a political philosopher writing from prison during the early 1930s, soon after Benito Mussolini's fascist regime gained control of Italy preceding World War II. Gramsci largely agreed with Karl Marx's proposal of communism as the best solution to global strife but found his expectation that capitalism would collapse, would be the final stage of empire, short-sighted. Capitalist oligarchies showed increasing sophistication at managing public dissent. They did this less through direct oppression than through psychological manipulation. Rather than

physically enforce their hegemony, except when absolutely necessary, they now endeavored to make

The world view of the ruling class...the 'common sense'
of the whole of society. Devices were employed such that
'... for the most part the ruling class did not have to resort
to force to maintain its dominance...' Gramsci thus had
the great merit of being the first Marxist theorist seriously
to analyze how the bourgeoisie managed to perpetuate
its domination through consent rather than coercion
(McLellan, 1979, pp.185-6).

In *A People's History of the United States* (1980), Howard Zinn observed that the nation's amazing free public
education system did not just teach students the skills
they needed to be well employed as adults. It also socialized them as to how to be good citizens in an appropriate
way. It sought, in fact, to mold virtually the entire labor
force of industrial America according to the values of the
mainly upper-class school boards across the nation.

It was important that these people learn obedience to au-
thority... [H]*istory was widely required in the curriculum to*
foster patriotism (p. 257).

Zinn perceived that much of history was purposely un-
taught. Vast portions were simply left out or distorted.
The fact that non-elite citizens without an accurate sense
of the past could hardly imagine ways to deal with their
present concerns, was not lost upon school boards.

In *Lies My Teacher Told Me* (1995), James Loewen reinforced Zinn's suspicions, listing specific examples of major history-distortions in virtually all high school textbooks.
Most striking was their common perpetuation of the myth
that Europeans conquered the Americas through their
skills of warfare and better technology, rather than as the
result of the diseases they brought with them, to which
they had grown immune, but to which New Worlders had

never been exposed. Implicitly, according to the textbooks, white people ruled the earth because they were
simply superior.

*By implying that no real questions about our future need
be asked and no real thinking about trends in our history
need be engaged in, textbook authors concede implicitly
that our history has no serious bearing on our future. We
can hardly fault students for concluding that the study of
history is irrelevant* (p. 263).

Media as a source of appropriate news

If the public assumed that one of public education's primary goals was to prepare young Americans from all social backgrounds for knowledgeable, intelligent, skillful,
participative citizenship in their democracy, it also assumed that newspapers and other media functioned to
keep them consistently well informed as adults, in service
of this same end. Noam Chomsky, one of the world's
leading linguists and political analysts, proposed in a
widely distributed 1984 essay that these understandings
were carefully constructed illusions. The actual goal of
upper-class policymakers was somewhat different. From

...the turn of the century until this day, [the public mind]
*was the object of a cultural and ideological industry that
was as unrelenting as it was diverse: ranging from the
school to the press to mass culture in its multitudinous
dimensions'* ... [In the United States] *Propaganda is to
democracy what violence is to totalitarianism. The techniques have been honed to a high art, far beyond anything that* [George] *Orwell dreamt of* (Peck, 1987, p.136).

in *Manufacturing Consent* (1988), Chomsky and a collaborator expanded upon this assessment.

*The mass media are not a solid monolith on all issues.
Where the powerful are in disagreement, there will be a*

certain diversity of tactical judgments on how to attain generally shared aims, reflected in media debate. But views that challenge fundamental premises or suggest that the observed modes of exercise of state power are based on systemic factors will be excluded from the mass media even when elite controversy over tactics rages fiercely (p. xi-xii).

Power lied more through the omission of real information than through the construction of false information, the authors perceived. They developed this thesis with examples revealing how U.S. foreign policy was systematically disguised from public view.

The power of the government to fix frames of reference and agenda, and to exclude inconvenient facts from public inspection, is... impressively displayed in the coverage of elections in Central America... and the analysis of particular cases in the chapters that follow (p. xiv).

In *Hegemony or Survival* (2003), Chomsky described what the media-created concept *spreading democracy*, which became popular during the 1980s, meant in Vietnam and Indochina. Ostensibly, it meant teaching and assisting Asian and other third-world governments (countries that during the cold war belonged neither to NATO nor the Warsaw Pact) how to turn from autocracy to democracy, through the electoral process. Chomsky perceived that consolidating U.S. political/economic control over targeted nations was spreading democracy's actual goal. Strategies included manipulating so-called democratic elections so that U.S. puppets were placed in office; and then the State Department getting itself invited to send advisors whose role had less to do with assisting in the management of a country's affairs, than in taking over their management. Violence, bribery, and subterfuge of all kinds were employed, under the auspices of the Central Intelligence Agency (CIA). In *Confessions of an Economic Hit Man* (2004), John Perkins described how as the employee of a consulting firm allegedly with strong governmental ties, he was employed to do just as Chomsky surmised. He persuaded nations to accept generous loans contrived to force them to become so heavily indebted to the lender as to be forced to operate in a manner consistent with U.S. interests in order to avoid being thrown into bankruptcy. As indicated earlier, the British had employed similar kinds of tactics prior to WWI, with disastrous results. Chomsky found these practices, less than a century later, to be dangerously irrational. Nothing highlighted this more than what finally came to light about the Cuban Missile Crisis, only long after the event.

[A] *possibly terminal nuclear war was barely avoided forty years earlier. Immediately after this startling discovery, the Bush administration blocked UN efforts to ban the militarization of space, as a serious threat to survival. The administration also terminated negotiations to prevent biological warfare and moved to ensure the inevitability of an attack on Iraq, despite popular opposition that was without historical precedent* (p. 2).

In *Rich Media, Poor Democracy* (1999), Robert Mc-Chesney, co-founder of Free Press, a national media reform organization, reinforced Chomsky's concerns. McChesney insisted that the public must become aware of what lies of omission hid from view: policy-makers' misdeeds, certainly, but also their lack of perspective beyond satisfying the narrow, short term needs of the U.S. ruling class — not unlike what had occurred in Egypt, Rome and other ancient empires.

We are in precipitous times. The corporate media system is consolidating into the hands of fewer and fewer enormous firms at a rapid rate, providing a hypercommercialized fare suited to wealthy shareholders and advertisers, not citizens (xxxiv).

...Capitalism benefits from having a formally democratic system, but capitalism works best when elites make most fundamental decisions and the bulk of the population is depoliticized. For a variety of reasons, the media have come to be expert at generating the type of fare that suits, and perpetuates, the status quo (p. 3).

Managing dissent, economically

In *The Populist Moment: A short history of the agrarian revolt in America* (1978), Lawrence Goodwyn described how economic devices were employed in a subtle and devious way to minimize organized public dissent. He found James Madison's prediction that when times became hard people would accept migration as a solution to their problems, and forego rebelling, to be accurate. Westward migration helped them very little, however, and as Hamilton had feared, they did not remain docile for long.

The nation's agriculturalists had worried and grumbled about 'the new rules of commerce' [which favored the rich] *ever since the prosperity that accompanied the Civil War had turned into widespread distress soon after the war ended. ...* [T]*hough railroad land agents created beguiling stories of Western prosperity, the men and women who listened and went, found that the laws of commerce worked against them just as much in Kansas and Texas as they had back home on the eastern side of the Mississippi River. ...* [They responded with] *the largest democratic mass movement in American history...* (pp. vii-viii).

Reforming federal bank policies became Populisms' primary goal.

Underlying the entire new structure of commerce was the national banking system, rooted in the gold standard and

*dominated by Eastern commercial banks, most promi-
nently the House of Morgan* (p. 70).

These banks heavily financed the rich while forcing small
property owners into bankruptcy, making them easy prey.
The big fish swallowed the smaller fish almost effortless-
ly. Populists' organized reaction to such abuse brought
about the creation of the Federal Reserve system in
1913, ostensibly a form of government protection from it.
In fact, it barely leveled the playing field at all. In *Secrets
of the Temple: How the Federal Reserve Runs the Country* (1987), William Greider described how the Federal
Reserve became an agency of enormous power, controlled by the rich and operating outside of the boundar-
ies of representative democracy —i.e., in secret.

*The Federal Reserve System was the crucial anomaly at
the very core of representative democracy, an uncomfort-
able contradiction with the civic mythology of self-govern-
ment* (pp. 11-12).

Goodwyn shared Greider's perception that owners of big
money controlled U.S. political and economic policy. Government agencies and programs purporting to ensure
equity among all property owners, whether very rich or
just getting by, left the dominance of the wealthy fully intact.

*The collective effect of twentieth-century agricultural leg-
islation — from the Federal Reserve Act of 1913 to the
abrupt ending of the Farm Security Administration's land
relocation program in 1943 — was to assist in the central-
ization of American agriculture at the expense of the
great mass of the nation's farmers* (Goodwyn, 1978, pp.
268-9).

Goodwyn described the crassness of the upper class, as
he perceived it, but also noted the apparent inability of
the public to grasp how U.S. democracy actually worked,

or to respond if they did grasp it, or to care enough to respond even when circumstances suggested that their efforts to improve their condition might be effective.

Populism never succeeded in attracting an urban audience, nor was urban labor well enough organized to respond to its socialist leanings in any case. ...[People fell into] *despair, grounded in the belief that hierarchical American society could, perhaps, be marginally 'humanized' but could not be fundamentally democratized...*(p. 270).

Managing dissent, politically

In *The Corporate Ideal in the Liberal State*: 1900-1919 (1968), published a decade earlier than Goodwyn's analysis, James Weinstein described how the Progressive Business Movement of Theodore Roosevelt managed social dissent with finesse rather than naked force. Where his predecessor, William McKinley, employed resources at his disposal to attack populist leaders in a harsh and often brutal manner, Roosevelt sought to co-opt them. His administration demonstratively embraced liberal policies and then manipulated these behind closed doors to further exclude small-property owners from participation in economic decision-making.

In short ... liberalism in the Progressive Era — and since — was the product, consciously created, of the leaders of the giant corporations and financial institutions that emerged astride American society in the last years of the nineteenth century and the early years of the twentieth (pp. xiv-xv).

A second challenge confronted Roosevelt-progressives when poor immigrants from Eastern Europe, many displaced by the failed revolutions of 1848 (about which more will be said shortly) brought Marxist and anarchist ideas to America.

*The 'growth of the Socialist party in this country,'
Roosevelt warned, was 'far more ominous than any populist movement in times past' (p.17).*

When workers reacted angrily to legislators' failure to en-
act meaningful worker compensation laws, threatening to
produce more labor-organizing than Roosevelt thought
healthy, he urged the business community to support
halfway measures, rather than rigidly oppose the workers' demands. Once passed, the more liberal-appearing
laws could be enforced in such fashion as to nullify their
purported intentions.

*This sweeping achievement was made possible by the
concerted activity of the National Civic Federation [NCF],
with the strong support of its big-business affiliates. It represented a growing maturity and sophistication on the
part of large-corporation leaders who had come to understand, as Theodore Roosevelt often told them, that social
reform was truly conservative (p. 61).*

Labor movements embracing socialist ideas, such as the
Industrial Workers of the World (IWW), and the Knights of
Labor, got sidestepped in favor of movements aligned
with capitalist-style democracy. These included the American Federation of Labor (AFL), and later the Congress of
Industrial Organizations (CIO). In concert with
Roosevelt's progressive-business strategy, the rising corporate community provided various kinds of welfare to
their employees, such as low-cost meals and entertain-
ments.

*... [P]aternalistic labor relations undermined union
strength and successfully forestalled the organization of
new unions. ...Much of the business support that was
given [Samuel] Gompers and the AFL was the result of a
widespread agreement in business circles to uphold conservative unionism... [Socialist] Eugene V. Debs [an IWW
founder] attacked Gompers... for bringing the AFL into*

*the NCF under the pretense that the workingmen had
friends among the industrialists ... (p. 21).*

The Discouragement of working-class organization became a National Civic Federation objective, and Ralph
Easely, its founder, worked hard to bring this about.

*[Easely] argued constantly for informal, which meant pri-
vate, attempts to reach compromises. ... [This meant]
keeping social questions out of the arena of public
debate...[From its inception, the NCF] tried to stabilize
the relationship between the workforce and corporate
enterprise. This entailed an insistence that trade unions
act responsibly, that they strictly adhere to and enforce
contractual agreements, even against the wishes of their
members. In effect, what the business leaders asked of
the conservative trade unionists was that they become
mediating agents between the workers and the corporations, rather than act simply as the representatives of the
workers in confrontation with their employers. In return,
NCF leaders sought to gain acceptance of organized labor as a permanent institution in American life and recognition for those labor leaders who would cooperate (pp.
31-8).*

The Sherman Antitrust Act of 1890 greatly assisted the
NCF to shift control of U.S. capitalism from the broad
confederations of laissez-faire capitalism, to the more
narrowly defined coalitions of corporate capitalism. Laissez-faire capitalism allowed anyone possessing property
to become an entrepreneur and take his best shot at
profiteering. Owners of property could combine their interests in any way they elected, including forming huge
cartels with which independent businesses could not
compete, and workers could not bargain. The Sherman
Act purported to put an end to such combines, on
grounds that they stifled free enterprise. Corporate capitalism, a new movement in the business community, narrowly defined combines of influence to include only men

of great wealth and prestige — in essence, the cream of the propertied class. Corporations differed little if at all from cartels in their effects upon free enterprise, but under Roosevelt's guidance the Sherman Act ignored their behavior and targeted only laissez-faire cartels.

Superficially and in the popular consciousness of small businessmen and farmers it was a mandate to prevent the spread of trust agreements and corporate consolidations... In fact, the Act had no such effect....By 1904 the top four percent of American concerns (the great majority of which were corporate in form) produced 57 percent of the total industrial output by value. By any standard of measurement, large corporations had come to dominate the American economy by 1904. How the judicial history of the Sherman Act accelerated and encouraged the consolidation of industrial enterprises into large corporations, in place of more informal, cartel-like arrangements between relatively small manufacturing concerns is a complex question... Essentially, the act was used by the Roosevelt administration only to break up business organization not controlled by NCF interests. ...Thus, despite Roosevelt's popular image as a 'trust-buster' his policy was that of accommodation to the large corporation system... (pp. 63-71).

Ten years later, in 1914, as discussed in part 9, World War I began, soon to be followed by a second world war, which did not end until the mid-1940s. These wars further enhanced the corporatization of the United States. Prominent progressive businessmen, supporters of Theodore Roosevelt, took control of what was called The War Industries Board (WIB). One prominent observer noted that it

'literally brought business into the business of Government.'...Some day, he mused, 'it may occur to some President to apply the organization scheme of the War Industries Board to Government'. Fourteen years

*later, during the crisis of the Great Depression Franklin
Roosevelt turned to [Bernard] Baruch for guidance* (pp.
214-233).

Franklin Delano Roosevelt (FDR), U.S. President from
1933-45, unlike Theodore Roosevelt (TR), his distant
cousin, was a Democrat. Nevertheless, FDR shared
TR'S view that enlightened businessmen should run the
nation. FDR felt closer to men like Baruch, one of the
country's wealthiest financiers and statesmen than to fellow democrats who saw men like Baruch as representatives of upper-class greed. Because of how Roosevelt
eased the terrible burden of the 1929-33 depression on
people's lives through agencies like the Works Progress
Administration and the Tennessee Valley Authority, both
of which provided government employment to people unable to find jobs, and extended social welfare beyond
anything so far experienced in the United States, he continues to this day to be regarded by many citizens, some
approvingly and some scathingly, as socialistic in his orientation. However, FDR did not oppose the severe inequalities of class division in U.S. society. He differed
from his wife, Eleanore, who urged him to assist working-
class citizens to establish themselves as a real force in
government. Like, TR, he viewed corporate capitalism
as an evolved form of elitism, capable of providing the
United States with a more functional ruling class than
had ever existed in the past.

*When the New Deal was over, capitalism remained in-
tact. The rich still controlled the nation's wealth, as well
as its laws, courts, police, newspapers, churches, colleges. Enough help had been given to enough people to
make Roosevelt a hero to millions, but the same system
that had brought depression and crisis — the system of
waste, of inequality, of concern for profit over human
need — remained* (Zinn, 1980, p. 394).

In *Who Will Tell the People* (1992), William Greider described how the Federal Reserve system was not the only regulatory agency that was formally created as a public servant but wound up serving the interests of wealth.

*The regulatory government is arguably the largest or second largest component in the political commerce surrounding the federal government, rivaled only by the defense sector in terms of the human and financial resources it consumes....During the 1930s, [Franklin] Roosevelt's New Deal created 42 major regulatory agencies and programs. Most of these involved economic regulation of specific sectors (airlines, broadcasting, oil and agricultural production and others), arrangements usually created in cooperation with the affected industries.
...[However] Instead of containing the political influence of concentrated economic power and liberating government from its clutches, the steady diffusion of authority has simply multiplied the opportunities for power to work its will* (pp.107-109).

The role of race in managing dissent

It has already been touched upon in this essay how ruling classes used divide-and-conquer as a way to stave off the emergence of organic solidarity among the lower classes of society. In the United States, it has involved differentiating the working class based on color. Lawrence Goodwyn described how during the populist movement, poor whites and blacks had begun for the first time to make common cause in seeking better treatment from employers. As a result, following the election of 1896, When Republican William McKinley beat Democrat William Jennings Bryan, white supremacy became a significant initiative of the Republican party.

[The]*victorious party of business had muted almost completely the egalitarian ideas that had fortified the party's early abolitionist impulses... Its prior political abandon-*

ment of black Americans had quietly become internalized into a conscious white supremacy. The word 'patriotic' had come to suggest those things that white, Protestant Yankees possessed. The Democratic Party was repeatedly charged with being 'too friendly' to foreigners, immigrants, and 'anarchists'.... [In particular] *the triumph of the business credo was matched, if not exceeded, by a conscious or unconscious internalization of white supremacist presumptions...* (Goodwyn, 1978, pp. 283-287).

NCF head Easley felt that anti-racism organizing within the black community could not safely be ignored. It had too much potential for gaining the support of all of the working class, meaning mostly white citizens. He wrote President Taft in 1909 when the National Association for Colored People (NAACP) was founded,

that 'this movement has been exploited by East Side papers for the past three months as a scheme to further Socialist propaganda.... Their theory is that there are 10,000,000 citizens who are being deprived of their constitutional liberties in this free land, and who would be willing to join any party or movement to stand for their rights' (Weinstein, 1968, p. 119).

Both Goodwyn and James Weinstein described how the white ruling class institutionalized racism as a way to demonstrate their supposed unity with the white working-class; to show that despite differences in wealth and opportunity, all white people possessed in common a fundamental kind of superiority. Oliver Cox, a black sociologist marginalized during his lifetime and currently viewed as one of the discipline's major theorists, developed this idea further. In an article published in the *Negro Journal of Education,* in 1945. Reviewing Gunnar Myrdal's classic study *An American Dilemma: The Negro Problem and Modern Democracy* (1944), Cox observed

how employers went to great lengths to create and reinforce division between the races.

[T]*he observed overt competitive antagonism* [between
races] *is a condition produced and carefully maintained
by the exploiters of both the poor whites and the
Negroes....It seems clear that in developing a theory of
race relations in the South one must look to the economic
policies of the ruling class, and not to mere abstract de-
pravity among poor whites... Moreover, it is not the poor
whites but the ruling class which uses its intelligence and
its money to guard against any movement among Negroes to throw off their yoke of exploitation* (pp. 23-5).

Cox described how this policy was designed far less to
make Negroes docile than to let whites know that they
would receive better treatment than blacks so long as
whites avoided organizing in opposition to their treatment
by employers. In *The Strange Career of Jim Crow* (1974),
Pulitzer Prize-winning historian C. Vann described an important part of the basis for this concern.

*It is altogether probable that during the brief Populist up-
heaval of the 'nineties Negroes and native whites
achieved a greater comity of mind and harmony of political purpose than ever before or since in the South* (p.
64).

In *Working Toward Whiteness: How America's Immigrants Became White* (2005), David Roediger described
how important it was to be defined as white if one wanted
to get ahead in the United States during the early Twentieth Century, when immigration from Europe shifted from
northern regions to southern and eastern countries. None
of these immigrants were automatically conferred white
status by immigration authorities, notwithstanding the col-
or of their skin.

[How] *Italian, Slav, Greek, German, French, Irish and other European races were gathered under the term 'Caucasian' in the twentieth century and thus unified as 'conclusively' white...*[is a story of] *messiness*] (pp. 8-9).

The problem was that many Eastern European immigrants brought socialist ideas with them to American shores.

In reflecting on a visit to her Hull House settlement by W.E.B. Du Bois, the social reformer Jane Addams suggested in 1909 that the interests and aspirations of the 'Mediterranean immigrants' attending did not include being white. They listened to the 'scholarly address' of the eminent African American intellectual and activist with 'respect and enthusiasm.' The Chicago Crowd watched with 'apparently no consciousness of the race difference which color seems to accentuate so absurdly.'... In the most ambitious early study of race in the United States, Swedish sociologist Gunnar Myrdal ... asserted that new immigrants held an 'interest in solidarity with Negroes' for a time after arrival or at least lacked 'the intense superiority feeling of the native Americans educated in race prejudice.' The very idea of securing a pure white, 'Anglo-Saxon' nation with such a diverse population could appear ridiculous to them (p. 95).

Roediger explained that such an attitude characterized many Italians, Poles, Jews, Irish, Greeks, and Armenians, all well educated in socialist theory and much more skilled than most U.S. working-class citizens at organizing and protesting against ill-treatment. However, they desperately needed U.S. citizenship and perceived how this could be jeopardized if they failed to conform.

In a nation that commonly denied citizenship rights and naturalization to those who were classed as not white... any enduring 'non-white' alliance would almost certainly have proceeded from an awareness of exclusion from the benefits of citizenship (p.121).

Thus, they learned to play the game: to embrace racism, and the hostility associated with it, in order to gain the acceptance they needed — not from people of their social class, but from powers that be who could either grant them acceptance or force them to return to their native countries. An article written by

Five leading historians ...[revealed how] *the new immigrants and the children of immigrants quickly learned that the 'worst thing one could be in this Promised Land was 'colored'* (p. 119).

During Franklin Roosevelt's liberal, democratic administration, federal agencies

actually ensured that new immigrants and their descendants would have less and less ability to choose to develop their own urban neighborhoods. New Deal housing policies empowered and advantaged new immigrants, but as whites, not as new immigrants (p. 231).

Defining oneself primarily as a member of a particular ethnic community, or even as a member of the working class, rather than as an individual white person seeking to become a U.S. citizen, was viewed as subversive and liable to jeopardize an immigrant's potential citizenship status. Even more so, asserting solidarity with members of the Nego community. By the end of World War I

The ghetto had unequivocally become black, and eastern and southern Europeans far more securely a part of the master race (p. 244).

In *Silent Covenants* (2004), Derrick Bell, Harvard Professor of Law and founder of the scholarly movement called Critical Race Theory, noted that acceptance of whiteness also meant acceptance of political docility— by white people.

The ideology of whiteness continues to oppress whites as well as blacks. Now, as throughout the American experience, it is employed to make whites settle for despair in politics and anguish in the daily grind of life. … [I]n a country that views property ownership as a measure of worth, a great many whites with relatively little property of a traditional kind… come to view whiteness as a property right….Given racism's critical role in providing an outlet for white frustrations caused by economic exploitation and political manipulation, one wonders whether American society could survive as we know it if large numbers of whites ever realized what racism costs them and decided to do something about it. (p.188)

In *The New Jim Crow: Mass Incarceration in the Age of Colorblindness* (2010), Michelle Alexander, a prominent black civil rights activist, documented how white privilege continued to be enforced as political policy.

The stark and sobering reality is that, for reasons largely unrelated to actual crime trends, the American penal system has emerged as a system of social control unparalleled in world history. And while the size of the system alone might suggest that it would touch the lives of most Americans, the primary targets of its control can be defined largely by race (p. 8).

Her study described in detail how criminal justice in the United States operates as a two-tiered system: one for whites, another for blacks, such differentiation being accomplished less by legislation than by differential enforcement of the law. Whites thereby received tangible economic benefits and immunity from oppressions that they might otherwise experience.

In *Escape From Freedom* (1970), social psychiatrist Erich Fromm observed that acceptance of ruling class gifts such as white supremacy benefitted citizens in some ways but damaged them in others. By prioritizing safety over decency, people cut themselves off from their inherent nature. They became easier to control.

The loss of the self has increased the necessity to conform ... [resulting in] the despair of the human automaton ... [and provides] fertile soil for the political purposes of Fascism (pp. 253-55).

Managing culture

The Psychological effects of racism upon white people may not have been an unintended byproduct of white supremacy supposedly designed to manage the working-class via an economic incentive. Throughout history, rulers appear to have feared and sought to undermine the emergence of organic solidarity as a driving force among the lower classes, by weakening them psychologically as well as physically. The possible roles of public education and journalism in this regard have already been noted. Another approach may have involved manipulating lower-class culture itself.

In *The Ministry of Culture* (1980), writer Michael Mooney described how in January of 1979, following a period of intense youthful activism during the 1960s and early '70s, a new agency came into being, responsive to president Jimmy Carter's feeling that the government should play a more active role in promoting the arts in the United States.

Our government needs to develop a rational, well-coordinated policy directed to the advancement and dissemination of the arts.... More effectively than weapons, more effectively than diplomacy, the arts can communicate, people to people, the spirit of America (p. 45).

Although the new agency was tied to official governmental bodies that were obliged to operate transparently, it provided no transparency itself.

The Federal Council on the Arts and the Humanities ... was an extraordinary institution. Seated in a long row behind their microphones at the High White Table of National Culture, the designated members of the Federal Council represented something more than was being admitted. ...[Here] sat commissioners, who said they were coordinating all national cultural policy, but there were few records of their achievements, nor any annotations of their purposes (p. 42).

In more than four hundred pages Mooney described how, in utter secrecy, Mondale's agency committed substantial energy and tax revenues to ensure that the "spirit" the president referred to would not include presentations that detracted from America's global image as a beacon of freedom, democracy, and opportunity. It accomplished this goal not by crushing such expression, but by funding art so heavily that artists did not need to reach out to their publics for support. Once the agency became the major source of funding, it firmly and quietly shut down art as an expression of community connectivity, of cultural richness, and of grassroots solidarity. Art was to be an act solely of individual expression.

The triumph of capitalism

It is important to note, in light of the foregoing segments, that most U.S. Americans embraced the stewardship of their capitalist ruling class, notwithstanding its excessive greed and ruthlessness from time to time. Perhaps the public was fooled by misinformation, propaganda, and journalistic lies of omission. Or maybe it just absorbed what it wanted to believe and denied the rest. A popular cartoon appearing in many newspapers during the early 1950s, called "Dogpatch", contained a character named

General Bullmoose (a euphemism for General Motors Corporation). His slogan was, "What's good for General Bullmoose is good for the U.S.A." Reportedly, Al Capp, the strip's creator, expressed amazement at how readily the public accepted such a claim.

On the other hand, maybe people just liked how the quality of their lives tangibly improved as subjects of the business class. No one has better documented the rise of capitalism as ideology than the highly acclaimed historian, and Marxist idealist, Eric Hobsbawm, who came under heavy criticism from socialist colleagues for the conclusions he felt forced by evidence to draw:

[Throughout Europe] *the situation of the labouring poor, and especially the industrial proletariat which became their nucleus was appalling between 1815 and 1848...* (1962, pp. 204-5). [However] *Eighteen forty-eight, the famous 'springtime of peoples', was the first and last European revolution ...The sudden, vast and apparently boundless expansion of the world capitalist economy provided political alternatives in the 'advanced' countries* (1975, pp. 2-3). *The known, mapped and intercommunicating area of the world was larger than ever before, its communications unbelievably speedier. ... Industrial production reached astronomic figures ... Science had never been more triumphant; knowledge had never been more widespread....Human invention was climbing more dazzling peaks every year....*[If] *the Industrial Revolution had created the ugliest world in which man has ever lived...*[and] *by uprooting men and women in unprecedented numbers and depriving them of the certainties of the ages, probably the unhappiest...* [and if no one] *could deny that there was poverty of the most shocking kind...*[not] *even the gloomiest of rational observers* [could] *maintain that in material terms it was worse than at any time in the past...* [Even] *the new socialists ... agreed that these were growing-pains.... [and] that human life faced a prospect of material improvement to equal the advance in man's control over the forces of nature* (1962, pp. 297-299).

Part 11: Disillusionment and Activism

The Muckrakers

As described in part 10, notwithstanding capitalism's attractions, during the late 1800s it produced enough discomforts to produce the Populist Movement. It also created a group of writers and journalists who scathingly critiqued the ills of the U.S. ownership class. These were the Muckrakers. During the late 1800s they gained a massive readership bringing into focus the

...pervasiveness of graft, the presence of a continuous corrupt connection between business and government, the link between government and vice... [Their books included] *W.T. Stead's If Christ Came to Chicago ...Henry Demarest Lloyd's Wealth Against Commonwealth...* [and Upton Sinclair's *The Jungle*. Journalists published in magazines with] *circulations running into the hundreds of thousands....* [There were newspaper crusades wherein] *Henry Adams and his brother Charles Francis ... muckraked the Erie ring and the 'Gold Conspiracy' ...*[T]*he New York Times, Harper's Weekly, and Thomas Nast ...*[went] *after Tammany in the* [eighteen] *seventies...*(Hofstadter 1955, 186-7).

President Theodore Roosevelt supported their efforts. As noted in part 10, He viewed rapacious business dealings as typical of laissez-faire capitalism, which he insisted must not be allowed to infect progressive corporate capitalism. He perceived that among the public

evil doing among the most respectable people is seen as the 'real character of American life; corruption is found on every side... If [however] *the laws are the right laws, and if they can be enforced by the right men, ...everything would be better* (203).

In other words, Progressivism meant firm elite control of the management of society in the spirit of a true Thomas Hobbesian social contract. This meant a ruling business class profiting, not through greedy exploitation of the populace, but the enhancement of America's progress and development as a great nation. If some pretense and misdirection concerning progressives' definition of democracy might come into play, this was not inconsistent with progressive ideology. James Madison had successfully argued at the Constitutional Convention that creating the illusion of democracy would serve better than nakedly asserting the full authority of those who must lead, as Alexander Hamilton insisted upon. Thus,

Theodore Roosevelt viewed the presidency 'as the steward of the public welfare...[wherein] 'the interest of the public is inextricably bound up in the welfare of our business.' Labor was thus bound 'not only by self-interest, but by every consideration of principle and duty' to stand with capital on 'matters of most moment to the nation.' (Williams, 391-2)

Most muckrakers objected not so much to capitalist elitism as to how this played out in the workplace and the marketplace. It was all right for bosses to hold the majority of power so long as they wielded it fairly. These reformers remained open to Teddy Roosevelt's progressivism so long as it bore fruit and produced changes. Some workers, however, began to wonder if the corruption of individual companies, cartels, and bought politicians brought into question the very nature of capitalism itself. This group gained strength from the influx of Southern and Eastern European immigrants brought up on Marxist communism. They called for the complete abolition of capitalism. Their ideas resonated even with workers who embraced and admired capitalism, as they increasingly felt betrayed by its current practices. Many whole-heartedly supported well-organized communists who pushed back aggressively against wage cuts and layoffs.

Communism also appealed to popular writers of the early twentieth century such as John Steinbeck, Richard Wright, John Dos Passos, Jack London, James T. Farrell, and others. If most citizens had no intention of signing on to communism, they did view it as a movement to be admired and taken seriously -- up until the early 1950s, when the disconnect between communism as ideology and its role as a mask for oppression in Russia became apparent (Harman, 2008, pp. 379-577).

In *Contours of American History* (1961), William Appleman Williams described how the communist critique of capitalism as a fundamentally undemocratic system undermined the muckraker perspective, which tended to perceive that it was only bad apples among the upper class who were responsible for their woes. Communists considered it absurd to imagine that once such individuals were set straight or removed from power things would improve. When Roosevelt's administration proved adept at absorbing exposes, promising change but moving only inches forward, over and over again, Muckrakers found it difficult to respond, and their resplendent moment of history came to an end (pp. 395ff).

Organized labor

In *The Age of Reform* (1955), Pulitzer-winning historian Richard Hofstadter described how U.S. involvement in WWI brought about a much weakened post-war economy from 1918 until the early 1920s. Democratic president Woodrow Wilson had insisted upon U.S. engagement in the war despite only modest public support, and he suffered a resounding defeat at the hands of Republican Warren G. Harding, in 1920. Under Harding, Theodore Roosevelt's progressive business ideology, which Wilson had fully embraced, crumbled. It became a transparent facade for greed. Under Calvin Coolidge and Herbert Hoover, it crumbled still further. Nevertheless, during most of the next decade, despite looming economic problems, the United States rebounded from postwar depression to become the richest, most technologically advanced nation in the world. This was "The Roaring Twenties," when the glass of progress and opportunity seemed more than half full notwithstanding nagging signs of ruling class degeneracy, and the lessening of capitalism in service of the community rather than of the very rich. On October 24, 1929 (Black Thursday), the economy collapsed with rippling effects spreading worldwide for a period lasting four years (pp. 284-86).

In 1937, the economy collapsed again, suffering its steepest ever decline. Sudden lay-offs of workers, wage cuts, and the brutal policing of protesters at the request of the wealthy class, led to the emergence of a new labor union. It consisted of a group of American Federation of Labor (AFL) members calling themselves the Committee of Industrial Organizations (CIO). Upon formally splitting with the AFL, they changed their name to Congress of Industrial Organizations. The CIO was communist-controlled, operated more aggressively than the ineffectual AFL (described in part 10), and for the first time in U.S. history dissolved racial inequality among its members. It quickly succeeded in forcing the huge General Motors corporation to come to the bargaining table, thereby gaining massive public acceptance and support. When the union next took on the steel industry, John L. Lewis, its leader, decided that it would be good strategy to identify fully with the democratic party of Franklin Roosevelt. He expected FDR'S full support. However, when union workers came under attack from hired thugs supported by both local and federal law enforcement, and Lewis beseeched Roosevelt for support, he was thoroughly ignored (Harman, 2008, pp. 512-19).

In 1941 Roosevelt brought the United States into WW II, and organized labor turned from protest to patriotism. This was not the first time that conflict between workers and employers had been set aside in such a fashion. A series of depressions beginning in 1913 had in every case been resolved through warfare, and each time with a significant strengthening of the corporate community. Theodore Roosevelt's Open-Door Policy and the Monroe Doctrine had rationalized aggressive U.S. foreign expansion on moral and ethical grounds—it was the "manifest destiny" of the United States to ensure that those whom God had designed to rule the world should do so—just when it could help the President avoid the consequences of a collapsing economy. So too did FDR's shepherding of the United State into warfare on similar grounds coincide with his need to pull the United States out of economic decline.

.[If] *entry into World War I was part of the transformation of American society ... involvement in World War II was the first phase of an era of fulfillment for the corporation society. ...[War] became the only policy that seemed practical — or moral.* (Williams, 1961, pp. 415-16).

Before the war, FDR had applied progressive ideology with great imagination to ease the burdens of the citizenry. He did this not by strengthening the public's ability to counteract the excesses of the upper class, however, but by pressuring the corporate community to operate with foresight, if not actual compassion.

In the years 1933-8 the New Deal sponsored a series of legislative changes that made the enactments of the progressive era [of Teddy Roosevelt] seem timid by comparison.... Above all, the New Dealers shared with the Progressives a far greater willingness than had been seen in previous American history to make use of the machinery of government to meet the needs of the peo-

ple and supplement the workings of the national economy (Hofstadter, 1955, p. 302).

This meant through corporate initiatives, rather than through the offices of civic agencies. Thus, FDR entrenched the Progressive Business Movement founded by TR by easing public discomfort without changing either the political or economic goals of the ruling class in any fundamental way. It took WWII, however, to pull the economy out of recession (Williams, 1961, pp. 343-469).

Following World War II came the Cold War, when at a certain point it appeared that Russia and the United States might engage in nuclear warfare (as described in part 9). During what historians label The Red Scare, from the late 1940s through the middle 1950s, people built underground nuclear fall-out shelters, and school children practiced crawling under their desks in case of nuclear attack. Any criticism of domestic or foreign policy that came across as too liberal was labeled communist, and came under harsh attack. Most liberals, including many who called themselves socialists, however, did not in any case embrace communism's endorsement of outright revolution.

In the U.S. the Taft Harley law required trade unions to purge Communist officials; government employees (including teachers and college lecturers) were sacked for refusing to sign 'loyalty oaths'; and directors and writers who would not denounce alleged 'Communist' contacts were banned from working in Hollywood by Senator Joe McCarthy's House Un-American Activities Committee... (Harman, 2008, p. 546).

Upon later examination, these extreme tactics had no relation to any real threat of organized treason. Contrary to what socialist idealists in the 1950s may have wanted to believe, in the final analysis,

Marxism had only a marginal effect upon the thought and action of… the great masses of Americans (Hofstadter, 1955, p. 326).

Nevertheless, the ideology of socialism continued to have appeal, not just in working-class circles but among the young middle class as well, and this worried higher-ups. Howard Zinn described how during the administration of Harry S. Truman, between 1952 and 1957

some 6.6 million persons were investigated. Not a single case of espionage was uncovered, though about 500 persons were dismissed in dubious cases of 'questionable loyalty' (1960, p. 420).

The progressivism of the two towering Roosevelts remained the dominant orientation of political/economic policy in the United States. It fulfilled the founding fathers' desire to create a system capable of sustaining elite control of U.S. society without resorting to more violence than was absolutely necessary. If corporate capitalism publicly espoused democratic ideology yet made sure that it could not truly manifest, if it limited public interference with elite policy in a multitude of ways, it somehow made its constant projections of community spirit believable.

In many respects, the Progressives tried to shield the governing decisions from what they regarded as the raw and ignorant passions of the public at large. The liberal intellectuals who came of age in the New Deal institutionalized the idea…notwithstanding that many were genuine reformers (Greider, 1992, p. 47).

The New Left

In *The Death and Rebirth of American Radicalism* (1996), Stanley Aronowitz described how 1960s reformers committed to improving U.S. capitalism joined forces with communists determined to destroy it.

Sometime in 1964 Jim [James] *Weinstein brought himself and the four-year-old Studies On the Left to New York from its birthplace in Madison, Wisconsin. The journal was started by students under the auspices of William Appleman Williams, a Wisconsin history professor who is now generally credited with having spearheaded the school of American historical writing called 'revisionism'. Williams, together with* [sociologist] *C.* [Charles] *Wright Mills, openly urged the generation of young intellectuals and political activists to break with all of the codes of traditional radicalism* [meaning revolutionary communism and anarchism] (p. 38).

Aronowitz, one of the new journal's editors, recalls how *Studies* strongly appealed to the left intellectual community made up mainly of university and college students. Weinstein and Aronowitz were staunch Marxists, but not so Willams and Mills. Both accepted reformers as potential agents of real change. Mills felt that they could be persuaded to see that their approach was not strong enough; that the existing ruling class could not be improved but must be removed from power. Williams considered the possibility that it could be improved, but his analysis of historical events failed to support such optimism. He concluded that World War II only masked the ineptitude of the progressive business movement to provide functional elite management of society.

...[I]n the single most crucial respect of creating a class-conscious industrial gentry capable and powerful enough to lead the system on a routine basis, the American political economy of the large corporation ... did not fulfill either its need or its logic.... [As] the dominant element in the political economy, the 20th century corporation did correspond to the lord of the manor in feudal society. Hence it was the institution to provide such a modern

gentry, and the system clearly needed the kind of informed and responsible leadership that the tradition was capable of providing [but did not] (Williams, 1961, p.454).

In *The Power Elite* (1956), Mills subjected the U.S. ruling class to a kind of surgical exposure. He began by observing that in democratic America some citizens possess greater policy-making power than others.

The power elite is composed of men whose positions enable them to transcend the ordinary environment of ordinary men and women...They form a more or less compact social and psychological entity...a social class (pp. 3-11).

In Mills' view, this was a class that assigned rights to itself not provided in the Constitution. It regarded the public as its subjects, basically. Constitutional rules and regulations presumably devices of public enhancement should be manipulated, as required, to ensure social control.

[They] *look upon 'the government' as an umbrella under whose authority they do their work* (pp. 255-287).

Mills viewed citizens as naively passive and easily molded, and the media and the public education system as designed to enhance these qualities.

The rise of the power elite ... rests upon, and in some ways is part of, the transformation of the publics of America into a mass society....[S]*ome of the higher agents of* [the] *media are themselves either among the elites or very important among their servants. ...'Democratic schools' often means the furtherance of intellectual mediocrity, vocational training, nationalistic loyalties, and little else* (pp. 297-320).

For all of its posturing, the power elite proved incapable of providing adequate social reasoning, Mills concluded, and this fact more than any should alarm the citizenry.

[W]*hat we are up against is a disinterest in and a fear of knowledge that might have liberating public relevance. ...*[M]en of decision enforce their often crackpot definitions upon world reality*....Commanders of power unequaled in human history, they have succeeded within the American system of organized irresponsibility* (pp. 356-61).

Mill's rhetorical style, and lack of attention to the achievements of capitalism, brought him the reputation of polemicist—not scientist — within the powerful mainstream sociological community. In *Masters of Sociological Thought* (1977), Lewis Coser devoted a few late paragraphs to Mills, describing him as nothing more than

... a belated offspring of midwestern populism... [whose] *The Power Elite (1956), presented a powerful challenge to much previous research in stratification and class analysis* (pp. 579-80).

Weinstein and other Marxist scholars applauded Mills' characterization of U.S. capitalism as fundamentally incompetent but deplored his acceptance of colleagues who embraced mere reformism as a way to deal with it. As it turned out, Mill's openness to all critics of capitalism resonated with a great many young intellectuals so far unaligned with any political organization. In 1960 he formulated his call to activism as a "Letter to the New Left," published first in the *New Left Review,* and subsequently in *Studies on the Left.*

...[W]*ho is it that is getting fed up? ...All over the world ...the answer's the same: it is the young intelligentsia...That's why we've got to study these new generations of intellectuals around the world as real live*

*agencies of historic change...Let the old men ask sourly,
"Out of Apathy- into what?" The Age of Complacency is
ending. Let the old women complain wisely about "'the
end of ideology.'"We are beginning to move again.
Yours truly,
C. Wright Mills* (Mills, 1960).

<u>Students for a Democratic Society, and Counter-Culture</u>

One member of the New Left with whom Mill's letter
strongly resonated was University of Michigan student
Tom Hayden. In 1959, together, with a few of his peers,
he endeavored to create a movement called Students for
a Democratic Society (SDS). Their goal was to expose
and confront capitalism's lack of decency and fairness,
especially its racism. Mill's letter prompted Hayden to
write an appeal that defined this focus. Presented at
SDS's first national conference, at Port Huron, Michigan,
in 1961, it became widely known as The Port Huron
Statement. Among other things, it asserted the following:

*We are the people of this generation, bred in modest
comfort, housed now in universities, looking uncomfort-
ably to the world we inherit.... As we grew... our comfort
was penetrated by events too troubling to dismiss. First,
the permeating and victimizing fact of human degrada-
tion, symbolized by the Southern struggle against racial
bigotry, compelled most of us from silence to activism.
Second, the enclosing fact of the Cold War, symbolized
by the presence of the Bomb...While these and other
problems either directly oppressed us or rankled our con-
sciences and became our own subjective concerns, we
began to see complicated and disturbing paradoxes in
our surrounding America....While two-thirds of mankind
suffers undernourishment, our own upper classes revel
amidst superfluous abundance. Although world population is expected to double in forty years... uncontrolled
exploitation governs the sapping of the earth's physical
resources....Our work is guided by the sense that we*

may be the last generation in the experiment with living. But we are a minority — the vast majority of our people regard the temporary equilibriums of our society and world as eternally functional parts. In this is perhaps the outstanding paradox; we ourselves are imbued with urgency, yet the message of our society is that there is no viable alternative to the present…. The search for truly democratic alternatives to the present, and a commitment to social experimentation with them, is a worthy and fulfilling human enterprise, one which moves us and, we hope, others today… On such a basis do we offer this document of our convictions and analysis…" (Ward, 2010, pp. 91-3).

Despite its small initial membership of only two hundred, SDS quickly became an influential movement.

By mid-April 1965, SDS was able to attract between 15,000 and 30,000 protesters to an antiwar rally in Washington, DC (Ward, 2010, p. 113).

Old-style socialists were impressed by its thrust and power but baffled by the energy SDS devoted to creating communal connectivity, rather than getting on with political strategizing and action. Aronowitz was stunned by *the primacy of the moral in SDS. it was the most articulate expression of what became the leading theme of the ideology of the 60s: the attempt to infuse life with a secular spiritual and moral content …*[SDS members shared] *the belief that they themselves were the new historical subjects.…Historians of this 'new left' have frequently mocked the SDS for spending the first half of any meeting adopting the agenda and defining the rules of debate, and even sympathetic observers have sometimes ascribed this strange ritual to inexperience or to the absence of a viable political culture. This criticism mis-understands the nature of the New left, summarized in a single word: process.… One worked out personal and procedural issues in great and often exhausting de-*

tail as a way of fusing the personal with the political, of creating a community not primarily of interest (political rationalism) but of feeling (pp. 30- 31).

Unfortunately, if the New Left espoused the values of organic solidarity, it did not entirely practice them. The movement included very few members of color, and though deeply motivated to

...assist the moral regeneration of the middle class.... to restore power to the person ...I cannot recall a single major woman figure in the early SDS, although women comprised a large proportion of the membership (pp. 5-46).

In parallel with SDS' growth, a movement of young people deeply disgusted and disillusioned by what they perceived as the flawed values of an adult community ready to sacrifice their children in a war upon Vietnam that had nothing, apparently, to do with upholding any reasonable moral code, as the government claimed, arose and flourished. Less politically strategic than SDS in its orientation, more philosophical, more emotional, and more poetic, this became known as the Counter Culture.

By 1965, 41 percent of the population was under 20 years of age... Young people were everywhere mobilizing against the draft or actually bearing the physical and emotional burden of fighting in Vietnam where the average age of combatants was 19; campaigning for civil rights; making and buying rock, folk, and soul music; experimenting with drugs and sex; tuning in and dropping out; but also getting educated in unprecedented numbers; spearheading new innovations in fashion, art, and culture; challenging conventional family and religious values; and exploring new avenues of spirituality (Ward, 2010, p. 9).

In *The Making of a Counter Culture: Reflections on the Technocratic Society and Its Youthful Opposition* (1969),

Theodore Roszak sought to give voice to the essence of their point of view.

So subtle and so well rationalized have the arts of technocratic domination become in our advanced industrial societies that even those in the state and/or corporate structure who dominate our lives ... [erroneously] see themselves as the conscientious managers of a munificent social system which is incompatible with any form of exploitation. At worst, [they imagine] the system may contain some distributive inefficiencies...[which] are bound to be repaired...in time (p. 9).

What young people understood for the first time in U.S. history, Rozak perceived was that the U.S. management elite rationalized a seriously dysfunctional society:

...a civilization sunk in an unshakeable commitment to genocide, gambling madly with the universal extermination of our species.... It insists, in the name of progress, in the name of reason, that the unthinkable become thinkable and the intolerable become tolerable. If the counter culture is, as I will contend here, that healthy instinct which refuses both at the personal and political level to practice such a cold-blooded rape of our human sensibilities, then it should be clear why the conflict between young and adult in our time reaches so peculiarly and painfully deep. In an historical emergency of absolutely unprecedented proportions, we are that strange, culture-bound animal whose biological drive for survival expresses itself generationally. It is the young, arriving with eyes that can see the obvious, who can remake the lethal culture of their elders, and who must remake it in desperate haste (pp. 47-8).

By 1968, college students' disillusionment with their ruling classes, and with the governments that served them, produced global reactions. Students in the metropolises of Europe, the United States, and Mexico protested against the unfair and inhumane practices of their elites. In the United States, for perhaps a decade, such disillusionment had been patiently accepted by officialdom, far more than working-class protests had ever been tolerated. But this came to an end on May 4, 1970, when

National Guard troops shot dead students at Kent State University in Ohio for protesting against President Nixon's extension of the Vietnam War into Cambodia (Harman, 2008, pp. 578-583).

To many analysts, this spelled the end of youthful activism.

Part 12: Activism Retreats and Grows

Following the killings at Kent State, a shock wave swept over the nation.

Four students were killed. One was paralyzed for life. Students at four hundred colleges and universities went on strike in protest. ... During that school year of 1969-1970, the FBI listed 1,785 student demonstrations, including the occupation of 313 buildings (Zinn, 1980, p. 481).

In 1965 sixty-one percent of the public favored U.S. involvement in Vietnam, but in 1970 the same percentage rejected it. This anti-war sentiment came not just from middle-class intellectuals and students, it expressed the view of the working class as well (pp. 482-3). But immediately following the shootings,

...a survey showed that three-quarters of Americans felt it was wrong to protest against the government and a large majority believed that in order to stop antiwar protests continuing, some of the basic freedoms secured by the Bill of Rights should be suspended (Ward. 2010, p. 207).

Stanley Aronowitz (1998) recorded that

By 1973, the New Left... was all but dead (p. 95).

Many found jobs within the conventional progressive liberal establishment. Others, like Tom Hayden,

worked as organizers and staff members for trade unions and liberal organizations or became activists in the Democratic Party... which grew progressively more conservative over the decades, not more radical (p. 92).

Small-movement activism

Activism did not die, however. Where large-scale movements had once occupied large public stages for many weeks and months, now small organizations began to occupy many small stages. Their focus was short-term and localized. Many of these identified with feminism, civil rights, and environmentalism.

Thus, when the media use the term 'left' they refer to the modern liberals, including the unions and the melange of single-issue and identify movements that have coalesced around the Democrats...(Aronowitz, pp. 122-3).

Aronowitz, a radical activist himself, had little faith in the ability of small single-issue movements to achieve much impact on U.S. politics and economy. He bemoaned the failure of large activism to hold on and persist. However, he came greatly to admire the contribution of 1960s counter culture to the way these movements operated.

The major contribution of the counter-culture ... was to have called attention to the politics of everyday life. And despite its many detractors, its influence remains and is perhaps, more enduring than that of the traditional lefts. It held before us a living vision of what a different, less stressed life might be like, it posed issues of equality in terms of the intimate details of daily living; and together with the new social movements, established, incontrovertibly, the salience of the politics of culture (pp. 186-7).

In *Direct Action: Protest and the Reinvention of American Radicalism* (2016), L.A. Kauffman, several decades younger than Aronowitz, but like him, an activist as well as a journalist of activism, viewed the retreat of the New Left in somewhat more generous terms than he did. Activism did not just spontaneously fade away, it was actively persecuted by powerful governmental agencies. Investigative journalists revealed the existence of

...vast FBI efforts under its COINTELPRO program to 'expose, disrupt, and otherwise neutralize the activists of the 'New Left' by counterintelligence methods,'... These and similar inquiries also uncovered a massive and illegal parallel program of domestic surveillance and infiltration by the CIA...(pp. 35-7).

She agreed with Aronowitz that 1960s counter culture played an important role in driving the evolution of small movement activism. Like small volcanoes, they erupted for a while and then faded from public view, usually leaving no long-term effect. On the other hand, there were a great many of them, and though each had its particular focus, movement organizers were not unaware of the big picture.

Anti-nuclear activists, for instance, weren't simply concerned with the health and safety risks posed by nuclear power plants; they viewed the push toward nuclear power as an outgrowth of a toxic ideology of 'progress' and 'growth' (pp. 43-5).

Furthermore, if activism had become decentralized, and if issues of focus had become diverse rather than unified, Kauffman perceived that the organizing skills of activists increased during this period. The importance of structuring activism as an egalitarian community process, rather than as a top-down political process was embraced by none more strongly than a particular group of anti-capitalists who had rejected both reformism and communism, and hence been marginalized during the '60s. These were the anarchists. While they agreed that capitalism could not be reformed, they disagreed with Marxists' insistence that the revolution needed to be carefully thought out, strategized, and managed by those most advanced in their knowledge and expertise. Anarchists were about spontaneity. Out of the ashes of torn-down capitalism would spontaneously emerge the system communists said they wanted. Kauffman came to the same conclusion that Aronowitz had voiced two decades earlier.

It was from the spirit of anarchism, not the doctrines of the conventional social justice left that one of the most widely influential new social movements of the post-war era, ecology, emerged.... What is profoundly radical about anarchism is its emphasis on the power of individuals and their communities to manage their relations to nature and between themselves autonomously. While the history of anarchism reveals important intellectual gaps and contradictions between theory and practice, its resolute critique of the state and its obsessive concern with domination is an indispensable antidote to the underlying authoritarianism of socialism and modern liberalism...(Aronowitz, pp.5-6).

Communists accused anarchists of ignoring how easily fascism can manipulate people seeking change when they have not yet grasped how their problems result not from elite practices, but from the very nature of elitism itself. Anarchists responded that installing a form of authoritarian leadership to bring about such understanding --what Marx called the dictatorship of the proletariat -- contradicted communists' professed ideology. Nearly all post-Marxist activists today agree with this argument, but insist that what they call praxis -- reading, debating, essentially thinking before acting, and re-thinking when action seems ineffective -- are crucial to bringing about rational social change.

Other demographics marginalized by '60s activism also rose to play a dynamic, formative role during the 1970s. Among the pioneers of what came to be called "identity politics" was the Combahee River Collective, a black lesbian and feminist group based in Boston (pp. 45-8).

Direct-action activism

Kauffman described how if some identity-based movements did lack vision, and did tend toward narrowness and fragmentation, others focused on how power was structured in the United States, and how to confront it effectively. One such movement was the Seabrook campaign of 1977, organized by the Clamshell Alliance. Their goal was to increase public awareness of the dangers of nuclear power, and they were able to make small waves that did not quickly dissipate. Two years later, when the nuclear power plant at Three Mile Island suffered a partial meltdown, their impact upon public sentiment expanded and strengthened substantially. Seabrook invited people not simply to come together in opposition to a social disfunction but to do this in a particular way.

The movements that created and refined the new model of direct action, from the anti-nuclear movement onward, weren't just seeking to create change through their protest activity; they sought to model, or prefigure, the world they hoped to create through the manner in which they organized. ... (pp. 57-9).

Direct actionists insisted, even more stubbornly than SDS had done during the 1960s, that establishing an organically solidary process of organizing must precede strategizing and activating. This orientation became widespread among identity-politics communities. In the mid-1980s, direct action took a particularly aggressive, in-your-face stance with a movement called ACT UP. Kauffman gave them top honors for good strategizing followed by effective action. A few similarly productive organizations spawned by ACT UP were Queer Nation, The Women's Action Coalition (WAC), the Lesbian Avengers, and Earth First.

The activists of this post-sixties generation were typically radicalized by the sense that their future was being foreclosed: by the threat of nuclear annihilation, ecological catastrophe, or government insolvency; by the erosion of abortion rights or the ravages of AIDS (pp. 88-90).

Collaboration and inclusion

Kauffman found that as single-issue activism became more aggressive it also became more collaborative. On April 25, 1995, a collection of racially diverse activists, from a variety of organizations, made common cause to shut down highway access to Manhattan in protest of the mayor's announcement of upcoming budgetary measures that would be particularly harmful to the working class. The activists had little impact on the city council's decisions,

but they accomplished something else: they modeled a new kind of direct-action-based, cross-racial political collaboration...(2017, p. 136).

In other words, small, well-trained, well-disciplined single-issue groups were gaining the ability to organize flexibly when they chose to. It happened again, on an even larger scale, when a confederation of organizations strove to shut down the 1999 World Trade Organization (WTO) meeting in Seattle. They perceived it as a major policy-making initiative that shut out and demeaned global working classes once again. From 1994 until 1999 an informal planning process created a loose network of confrontations. They could not shut down the meetings, but still produced significant results beyond anyone's expectations. All of this came as the result of the voluntary, and loosely organized collaboration of single-issue groups.

[T]here was a powerful and unmistakable alchemy as they combined. ... (pp. 143-7).

What was missing from Seattle was any substantial involvement of people of color. This changed in 2000 when mixed-race protesters filled New York City streets in protest of the acquittal of police officers who had killed Amadou Diallo, an unarmed young Guinean immigrant whom police later said they had mistaken for someone suspected of a rape committed the previous year. Direct action communities of color have since gained increasing strength and sophistication in pushing back against what has been called the prison-industrial complex in the United States.

The 2001 IMF(International Monetary Fund)/World Bank meetings were the next big direct-action target. The antiwar movement organized by UFPJ (United for Peace and Justice) that developed in opposition to the Bush administration's intention to use 9/11 as the excuse to invade Iraq, would lead the confrontation. This would surely have furthered cross-racial collaboration had 9/11 not occurred. Following the destruction of the World Trade Center, activist militancy became unthinkable to most citizens, hence the UFPJ adopted a less confrontational approach than it had intended. The president simply ignored it (pp. 162-7).

Occupy Wall Street

Kauffman described how five years later activism shifted again, coming full circle to C. Wright Mills' invitation to the New Left to focus less on the particular inequities of the ruling class, and more on the question of its fundamental ability to create social stability of any kind. In 2008, Barack Obama's campaign for president awakened and inspired many of the nation's young to actively seek social changes offering hope for a future defined by more social justice and basic kindness. As the worst recession since the 1930s kicked in, their anger at the wealthy class gave rise to a small group in New York determined to confront Wall Street directly. They wanted answers to why the nation's business class, especially the financial sector operated as it did. Blocked by police from access to the New York Stock Exchange, they decided to hunker down in nearby Zucotti Park, and remain there until Wall Street responded. Their example became a tipping point, and Occupy Wall Street (OWS) was born. Across the nation groups formed and sat themselves down as close to financial centers and City Halls as possible in a fashion that was unprecedented:

[They] *declined to spell out concrete demands or goals....* [OWS's] *signature political move was... sparking sustained debate about what a radically transformed egalitarian society might look like. ...* (2017, p. 169).

Convinced that American democracy had become dysfunctional, OWS members were not certain exactly how to define and analyze their concern, or how to engage the ruling class once they did so. Their discussions took the views of everyone seriously, including reformists, communists, anarchists, and people with no defined political orientation. Rather than select one or another perspective, or some amalgam of perspectives quickly, they preferred to pursue a process of dialogues and multilogues, lasting as long as necessary, until consensus was achieved. Building the movement took precedence over getting things done quickly. This did not sit well with anarchists who insisted that spontaneous action was more functional than discussion. Other kinds of issues arose as well, such as health problems, neighbors objecting to evening drum circles popular among some of the Occupy groups, and police encouraging people addicted to drugs and alcohol, living on the streets and in need of food and shelter, to join the OWS encampments. Finally, the encampments' sanitation issues made them easy targets for eviction.

Black Lives Matter

Occupy's commitment to racial inclusion left something to be desired and drew criticism from activists of color. Nevertheless, its organizing approach enhanced the expansion of anti-racist activism. When black teenager Trayvon Martin was murdered on February 26, 2012, by a white vigilante, with no response from the State's criminal justice system, an organization called Dream Defenders formed and encamped in front of Florida's capital, OWS style. Two years later

In the summer of 2014, people poured into the streets of Ferguson, Missouri after a white policeman shot an unarmed black teenager in the back — the tip of the iceberg of black abuse by Ferguson police over a period of many years — and stayed there for many days. A well-established organization in St. Louis called Organizing for Black Lives (OBL), together with a smaller organization that had participated on the Occupy Wall Street campaign, quietly went into fast action to provide support to the protestors. They set in motion a nationwide upsurge of organizing for black lives (Kauffman, p. 175).

This was the beginning of Black Lives Matter.

Big Organizing

In Rules for Revolutionaries (2015), Becky Bond and Zack Exley, two experienced organizers who shared the OWS perspective, described how they came remarkably close, against powerful odds, to transforming the U.S. Democratic Party. They nearly succeeded in enabling an aggressive left-wing reformer, Bernie Sanders, rather than a moderate, establishment-supportive centrist, Hillary Clinton, to represent the Party in the 2016 U.S. presidential election. Sanders challenged the way the Democratic National Committee (DNC), essentially the Party's power elite, had for decades served the interests of the U.S. management class more than the interests of working-class citizens, who were the party's alleged ideological charges. He did not expect the party to reject capitalist elitism but insisted that it must nevertheless operate in the interests of all U.S. citizens, especially including people of color. Clinton did not basically disagree with Sanders but felt, in concert with the DNC, that his extremism would alienate many democratic voters who accepted conservative neoliberalism, more than they accepted progressivism. In any case, Republicans, in Clinton and the DNC's view, were far far worse in their treatment of people than democrats had ever been, and this is what must be gotten across in the next presidential election.

Bernie began the race fairly late in the game, with 3 percent name recognition, no money, and all kinds of baggage that pundits believed would disqualify him out of hand... (p.183).

No one thought he had a chance against Hillary Clinton. His campaign headquarters determined to put him forward as inexpensively as possible, hoping for but not counting on a miracle. Bond and Exley were hired to recruit as many volunteers as possible to create a campaign presence in states that would not be supplied with paid staffers until the campaign was well underway, and perhaps only a token few even then if the campaign was going nowhere. No one anticipated what Bond and Exley would accomplish. Among other things, the

...Bernie campaign raised over $231 million from 2.8 million individual donors (p. 64).

Their orientation from the beginning was typical of direct activism:

Bernie Sanders wasn't the movement. He was in the movement (p. 159).

What they meant by this was that their goal was not simply to elect a good political candidate, but to get a left-wing activist movement into office. Sanders was someone who if elected and held accountable, would serve well enough. The movement would support him; but it would also guide, mold and, if necessary, control him. Calling upon their previous experience and contacts, the two assembled a small group of highly competent colleagues, most professional organizers themselves, who quickly constructed a database containing emails and phone numbers of potential volunteers willing to do whatever it took to raise money for Sanders and get out the vote for him. Many of the contacts in the data based were provided by a group called People for Bernie, which had been organized by two activists who had accumulated data on a million people who liked Occupy Wall Street on Facebook.

[People for Bernie's] *social media content hit timelines literally billions of times... [creating] an important counterbalance to the corporate mainstream media that essentially ignored the Bernie campaign for much of the cycle* (p. 94).

The organizers' next step was to ensure that their colleagues, many of whom were eager to create events of their own design, would instead commit to a single centralized strategy. After some discussion, the team accepted Bond's insistence that

... [w]hen it comes to moving voters to the polls in elections... the gold standard ... is a volunteer having a conversation with a voter on the doorstep or on the telephone (p. 4).

We believed we could create a capacity to make millions of calls.... But no one had ever done this at scale in a primary before...(p. 55).

This meant that someone must coordinate and manage not a few, but a large number of volunteers, which was usually a function of paid staff, and there was no money for this. It was as though a farmer had produced a bumper yield of crops but lacked the funds to harvest it. As it turned out, their worries were groundless. The number of volunteers responding to the team's initial outreach possessed of direct-action background stunned Bond and Exley. Some had as much or more experience than they did. There were more than enough of these super-volunteers to coordinate a mass of other volunteers. It turned out that paid staff were hardly needed at all. However, persuading the super-volunteers to follow the procedures Bond and Exley had worked out for staffing and managing phone banks, was not easy. Getting them on board, individual by individual, would take too long, and so Exley came up with an idea: the team would hop -- barnstorm -- from location to location across the country conducting intensive education and training workshops with a few hundred people, packed into an intense day or so. This proved immensely successful.

We considered the barnstorm meeting the most valuable innovation devised by our department over the course of the campaign. (p. 81) ...If we had started earlier and figured out barnstorming earlier, we would have had a much larger capacity ...(p. 143).

In the final analysis, while

Hillary Clinton's primary campaign struggled to get a handful of events planned by volunteers on her website ... Bernie had thousands (p.15) ... [By the end of the campaign] more than one hundred thousand volunteers had made calls to voters...They made more than seventy-five million calls.... More than one hundred thousand volunteer-led 'events' were held, and more than one thousand 'barnstorm' mass meetings were led... (pp 2-3).

Bond and Exley surmised that Bernie would have won had they begun earlier, especially had they begun barnstorming earlier, and been allowed by the Sanders campaign heads a freer hand. Their greatest regret was that race as an issue tended to lose rather than gain focus during the campaign.

Without truly multiracial solidarity, we simply won't be able to build a political revolution big enough to win real change in the United States (p. 39).

As of this writing, direct action and big organizing are steadily more integrated and more racially and sexually diverse. If activism still seems over wedded to single issues, its potential for morphing into something grand and overarching seems only to grow.

Part 13: Can Elitism be Improved?

Most scholars and most citizens have regarded elitism as needing improvement, but not abolishment. Some basically agree with Thomas Hobbes. Social stability requires firm, if not ruthless guidance from a superior individual or power elite. Others advocate for at least a measure of citizen participation in the formation of social policy. Still others place very little faith in existing power elites but doubt that full democracy can be achieved in modern complex society. Parts 10-12 presented some evidence of ruling class deficiencies, but the only analysts discussed so far in this essay who have challenged the feasibility of elitism at all as a way for human beings to thrive were Karl Marx, in part 7, and Charles Wright Mills, in part 11. The segment that follows presents further scholarship that raises this question. The next segment features an examination of perhaps the most extensive advocation of elitism in history: a two-volume work of more than a thousand pages by Pulitzer prize-winning social-psychologist Steven Pinker.

Might elitism be fundamentally inadequate?

Herbert Marcuse, sociologist and philosopher, a member of the prestigious Frankfurt School of Sociology and an icon of counter-culture activism during the 1970s, began One Dimensional Man (1972), with a disturbing question.

Does not the threat of an atomic catastrophe which could wipe out the human race also serve to protect the very forces which perpetuate this danger?....[M]ass media have little difficulty in selling particular interests as those of all sensible men... and the whole appears to be the very embodiment of Reason. And yet this society is irrational as a whole. Its productivity is destructive of the free development of human needs and faculties, its peace maintained by the constant threat of war, its growth de-

pendent on the repression of the real possibilities for pacifying the struggle for existence...(p. ix).

In other words, the illusion of ruling class competence, sold by elite-controlled mass media has grown wafer-thin. The dangers of societal collapse have become all too real.

Independence of thought, autonomy, and the right to political opposition are being deprived of their basic critical function in a society which seems increasingly capable of satisfying the needs of the individuals through the way in which it is organized (pp. 1-2).

In other words, this imminent social collapse, orchestrated by ruling classes, occurs in societies well enough advanced to provide citizens with a decent quality of life. Yet too many people accept the illusion of elite competence.

It was this fact that concerned Marcuse the most. In the rest of One Dimensional Man Marcuse described and tried to make sense of such entrenched complacency. He concluded that it was very problematic, but also superficial. Marcuse placed no faith in ruling classes' ability to evolve, to become more rational, but perceived that the masses of citizens could do so. In the United States, at least, citizens' denial of reality, their rationalizing of conformity in exchange for jobs, their acceptance of mechanical-solidarity as a normal process, in short, their socially-constructed one-dimensionality, could be dispelled. People could wake up and reverse current trends. They could put an end to five millennia of elitist irrationality.

Underneath the conservative popular base is the substratum of the outcasts and outsiders, the exploited and persecuted of other races and other colors, the unemployed and unemployable. They exist outside the [illusory] dem-

ocratic process... and therefore possess the potential to provide an elementary force which violates the rules of the game, and in doing so, reveals it as a rigged game. ... Should they exercise this potential, start refusing to play the game this may mark "the beginnings of the end of a period (pp. 256-7).

Erich Fromm, Frankfurt School social psychologist and Marcuse's colleague, shared his critique of elitism as fundamentally incompetent and socially destructive. In Escape From Freedom (1979), Fromm expressed concern, however, that people might no longer be capable of responding to this threat. He feared that adapting to elite rule for five thousand years might finally have disabled the lower classes' ability to strive for organic solidarity.

[T]he drive for freedom inherent in human nature, while it can be corrupted and suppressed, tends to assert itself again and again....[However] traumatic social conditions, such as totalitarianism, could short circuit this drive (p. xv).

Fromm perceived that many citizens no longer strove to self-actualize.

We have become automatons who live under the illusion of being self-willing individuals (p. 252).

Passive conformity had become rationalized as necessary; dis-obedience was no longer a personal choice.

The feature common to all authoritarian thinking is the conviction that life is determined by forces outside of man's own self, his interest, his wishes. The only possible happiness lies in the submission to these forces... The essence of the authoritarian character has been described as ... [seeking] unrestricted power over another person more or less mixed with destructiveness... [or]

*dissolving oneself in an overwhelmingly strong power
and participating in its strength and glory* (p. 169).

As noted previously, in the early 1930s Antonio Gramsci
had predicted that modern capitalism would use techniques of propaganda and misdirection to maximize ruling class control of society, allegedly for the people's
own good. Fromm surmised that with effort people might
identify and then reject their self-alienation, and break
free of elite control. However the first step must occur
before the second could be achieved. For Fromm, as for
Marcuse, this meant transforming self, and then society.

*Only if man masters society and subordinates the eco-
nomic machine to the purposes of human happiness and
only if he actively participates in the social process, can
he overcome what now drives him into despair...[He
must embrace] freedom as the active and spontaneous
realization of the individual self* (p. 274).

Fromm, like Marcuse, perceived the only hope for the
emergence of sound social reasoning to inhere in people's ability to rid themselves of their addiction to elite
rule, because the elite could not heal itself of its illness.
Both public and elite were infected by a social pathology
that he termed authoritarianism -- which will receive further discussion in part 14.

Thomas Piketty, prize-winning economist, reinforced
Fromm's concerns. In Capital in the Twenty-First Century
(2014), he described how capitalism created extreme
social inequality that he found to be dysfunctional and
ultimately irrational. But it was not this oligarchic behavior that most disturbed him. It was how capitalism no
longer enhanced society in the process of enriching the
upper class.

*[I]n a democracy, the professed equality of rights of all
citizens contrasts sharply with the very real inequality of*

living conditions, and in order to overcome this contradiction it is vital to make sure that social inequalities derive from rational and universal principles rather than arbitrary contingencies. Inequalities must therefore be just and useful to all... (p. 534).

And this was not the case.

One of the most striking lessons of the Forbes rankings is that, past a certain threshold, all large fortunes, whether inherited or entrepreneurial in origin, grow at extremely high rates, regardless of whether the owner of the fortune works or not (p. 556). Once a fortune is established, the capital grows according to a dynamic of its own, and it can continue to grow at a rapid pace for decades simply because of its size (p. 575).

Unless these monies are reinvested,

...no matter how justified inequalities of wealth may be initially, fortunes can grow and perpetuate themselves beyond all reasonable limits and beyond any possible rational justification in terms of social utility. Entrepreneurs thus tend to turn into rentiers not only with the passing of generations but even within a single lifetime...(p. 562).

Put simply, the wealthy class was no longer reinvesting its wealth. It was living off the interest created by the wealth. This meant that new factories, new technologies, and most importantly new jobs were not being created. This rentiership set in motion

an oligarchic type of divergence, that is, a process in which the rich countries would come to be owned by their own billionaires or, more generally, in which all countries, including China and the petroleum exporters, would come to be owned more and more by the planet's billionaires and multimillionaires (Piketty, p. 588).

The entrepreneur as rentier inevitably becomes *more and more dominant over those who own nothing but their labor ...[and] capital reproduces itself faster than output increases.... [The] consequences for the long-term dynamics of the wealth distribution are potentially terrifying. The right solution is a progressive annual tax on capital* (pp. 746-7).

Failing this, capitalism can no longer constitute a force of social progress or guarantee social stability of any kind. Piketty did not advocate for revolution, but he did express alarm that capitalism seemed fatally ill at the time of his writing and seemed unable to heal itself.

Joseph Stiglitz, a Nobel prize-winning economist, perceived additional indications of elite irrationality. In Globalization and its Discontents (2003), written while he served as chief economist and senior vice president of the World Bank, he observed that

globalization — the removal of barriers to free trade and the closer integration of national economies — can be a force for good. [It has] the potential to enrich everyone in the world, particularly the poor.... [Unfortunately] the way globalization has been managed, including the international trade agreements that have played such a large role in removing those barriers and the policies that have been imposed on developing countries in the process of globalization, need to be radically rethought...[He observed that] decisions were often made because of ideology and politics. As a result, many wrong-headed actions were taken, ones that did not solve the problem at hand but that fit with the interests or beliefs of the people in power (pp. ix-x).

The inconsistency between these entrenched interests and beliefs and the stated goals of the World Bank and the International Monetary Fund (IMF) created a disturbing anomaly.

The fact that a lack of coherence has led to a multitude of problems is perhaps not surprising. The question is, why the lack of coherence? Why does it persist, on issue after issue, even after the problems are pointed out? Part of the explanation is that the problems that the IMF has to confront are difficult... But I think there is a more fundamental reason: The IMF is pursuing not just the objectives set out in its original mandate... it is also pursuing the interests of the financial community....[This] new mandate had to be clothed in ways that seemed at least superficially consistent with the old (pp. 206-7).

Simple greed or opportunism might have explained these inconsistencies, but Stiglitz found no evidence that even such crass purposes were served by the incompetencies he observed. He wound up genuinely amazed that well-educated, bright administrators, and their supervisors, mindlessly hewed to such unproductive norms of behavior. He was alarmed at what this implied.

Globalization today is not working for many of the world's poor. It is not working for much of the environment. It is not working for the stability of the global economy (p. 214).

E.O. Wilson, social-biologist and ecologist mentioned frequently in this essay, twice Pulitzer Prize winner, cast elitist environmental policy in a light similar to what Stiglitz' revealed. In the concluding section of Consilience (1998), he observed:

Few will doubt that humankind has created a planet-sized problem for itself. No one wished it so, but we are the first species to become a geophysical force, altering Earth's climate...the greatest destroyer of life since the ten-kilometer-wide meteorite that landed near Yucatan and ended the Age of Reptiles sixty-five million years ago...(pp. 277-8).

In other words, humans have reduced the number of other animal species in the world to a potentially catastrophic degree.

It is notoriously difficult to estimate the overall rate of extinction, but biologists, by using several indirect methods of analysis, generally agree that on the land at least, species are vanishing at a rate one hundred to a thousand times faster than before the arrival of Homo sapiens.... The more species that live in an ecosystem, the higher its productivity and the greater its ability to withstand drought and other kinds of environmental stress. Since we depend on functioning ecosystems to cleanse our water, enrich our soil, and create the very air we breathe, biodiversity is clearly not something to discard carelessly... In this matter the opinion of biologists and conservationists is virtually unanimous. The only way to save the Creation with existing knowledge is to maintain it in natural ecosystems. Considering how rapidly such habitats are shrinking, even that straightforward solution will be a daunting [but not impossible] task (pp. 293-97).

In the preceding sections of Consilience (as noted in part 7) Wilson focused on how the decision-making skill of a modern human community bore upon its thriving. Like many other skills, this one too was subject to natural selection. This occurred not biologically, however, but culturally. Communities that invented the most adaptive techniques, or copied them from others, thrived best. Virtually all cultures honored old traditions, but when these lost their functionality successful communities could modify or discard them. Failure to succeed at good-enough decision-making spelled likely extinction. Wilson ended Consilience with concern that this was not a theoretical possibility at the time of his writing, but a very real one.

To the extent that we depend on prosthetic [technological] devices to keep ourselves and the biosphere alive, we will render everything fragile. To the extent that we banish the rest of life, we will impoverish our own species for all time (p. 298).

Hope Jahren, prize-winning Paleobiologist, reinforced Wilson's fear, but also his perception that the future was not yet hopeless -- in The Story of More (2020).

The 'father of biodiversity,' E.O. Wilson, is now promoting the ideal of the 'half-earth' —a full 50 percent of the earth's land to be designated a human-free natural reserve…. These are the types of measures needed if we hope to prevent a sixth mass extinction during the next several centuries…The good news is that there is no reason to think that energy conservation will necessarily reduce our quality of life… Indeed, if we look at the most comprehensive measures used to estimate the elusive concept of 'happiness,' we find that our increasing consumption of food and fuel over the last decade [in the U.S.] has not made us happier — quite the opposite. In 2017, the Global Happiness Council, a group headed by United Nations adviser Jeffrey Sachs, reported that Americans were the unhappiest they had ever been, at least since 2005, despite the fact that they were working, eating, and consuming more than ever before….[On the other hand] it's no use pretending that conserving resources isn't at direct odds with the industries that helped to write our Story of More and that increasing consumption over the last fifty years wasn't coupled to the pursuit of more profit, more income, more wealth (pp. 167-70).

In short, life-saving environmental policy, which should not be all that difficult to implement, or all that painful to live with, has little chance of emerging so long as those with the greatest decision-making power oppose it. Implicitly, better deciding is required. How to bring this about Jahren does not address.

Jared Diamond, Pulitzer prize-winning geographer, described in Collapse (2011) how several post-agricultural-revolution societies fell prey to environmental threats that should not have brought about their downfall. He endeavored to find out how this came about.

For the first time in history, we face the risk of a global decline. But we also are the first to enjoy the opportunity of learning quickly from developments in societies anywhere else in the world today, and from what has unfolded in societies at any time in the past That's why I wrote this book (p. 24).

He wound up astonished at how many societies collapsed as the result of irrational decision-making by ruling classes in full possession of information they could have used to avoid disaster -- a phenomenon still well in evidence across the globe.

Our world society is presently on a non-sustainable course, and any of our 12 problems of non-sustainability that we have just summarized would suffice to limit our lifestyle within the next several decades. They are like time bombs with fuses of less than 50 years... [W]e shall have depleted or destroyed most of the world's remaining fisheries, depleted clean or cheap or readily accessible reserves of oil and natural gas and approached the photosynthetic ceiling within a few decades (p. 498).

More than any scholar, Diamond produced empirical evidence of irrational social policy directly related to community thriving -- always under the control of a ruling class. Whether the problem was elitism itself, or malfunctions of elitism requiring attention and repair, he did not address, but some reviewers of his work perceive that he leaned toward the latter view. Perhaps despite its malfunctions, without elite management of society, we would be much worse off than we are; notwithstanding the near hundred percent probability of an impending extinction event unless the environmental policies of global power elites change quickly.

Is elitism both adequate and necessary?

In The Better Angels of Our Nature (2011) and Enlightenment Now (2018), each study comprising more than 500 pages, Steven Pinker makes precisely this assertion. Early in the first volume, he states his connection with Thomas Hobbes and his embrace of Leviathan, a human sovereign emulating the Old Testament sea monster possessed of enormous strength and wrath, but also wisdom.

Hobbes's analysis pertains to life in a state of anarchy. The title of his masterwork identified a way to escape it: The Leviathan, a monarchy or other government authority that embodies the will of the people and has a monopoly on the use of force. ...Archaeologists tell us that humans lived in a state of anarchy until the emergence of civilization some five thousand years ago, when sedentary farmers first coalesced into cities and states and developed the first governments. If Hobbes' theory is right, this transition should also have ushered in the first major historical decline in violence (2011, p. 35).

As noted in part 3, anthropologists and archaeologists now find this assessment to be controversial, if not flat-out wrong. They agree that internal violence plagued human communities beginning five to seven thousand years ago but probably occurred pretty rarely during most of the more than a hundred millennia before that. Pinker does acknowledge that while citizens of modern societies are constrained by law from aggressing against one another, or against their State, this does not apply to the State's right to operate violently whenever it wishes to.

[T]he first Leviathans solved one problem but created another. People were less likely to become victims of homicide or casualties of war, but they were now under the thumbs of tyrants, clerics, and kleptocrats....Solving this second problem would have to wait another few millen-

nia, and in much of the world it remains unsolved to this day (2011, p. 58).

Despite this issue, and without examining its current implications, Pinker flatly reasserts that the trend of Leviathan has been more beneficial than destructive. Resisting its civilizing influence is therefore irrational. While activism of the 1960s usefully exposed ruling-class greed and inhumanity, it also, and more importantly, glossed over social advances attributable to elitism.

[O]ne of the side effects was to undermine the prestige of aristocratic and bourgeois lifestyles that had, over the course of several centuries, become less violent than those of the working class and underclass. Instead of values trickling down from the court, they bubbled up from the street.... These currents pushed against the civilizing tide in ways that were celebrated in the era's popular culture... (2011, p. 110).

Pinker does not reference, much less refute scholars such as those referred to in the previous section of this part as well as in part 10, who proposed that ruling-class strategies of social management tended to diminish social progress and social stability. He lumps all criticisms of elitism under the rubric "progressophobia," where he makes a brief but interesting case that critics of Leviathan are motivated not by good science, but by a kind of fashionable obstructionism (2011, p. 214-15ff).

If Pinker's disregard of scholarship challenging his thesis reflects poorly on his objectivity, how many of his peers maligned Pinker's seminal work, The Blank Slate, upon its publication in 2002, reflects just as poorly on theirs. In contradiction of prevailing public opinion and that of much of the academic community, Pinker rigorously demonstrated that nature figures as importantly as nurture in defining human nature -- our genetic hard-wiring counts as significantly as what we are taught. Immediately he

found himself awash in accusations of aiding and abet-
ting racist fascism, which rested on just this premise.
Subsequently, science thoroughly undermined the supposed biological validity of racism and The Blank Slate
now ranks as a seminal contribution to knowledge. But at
the time, Pinker received little support from his peers for
what was a perfectly valid, and as it turned out accurate
hypothesis.

Pinker's suspicion concerning the objectivity of anti-elit-
ists, who appear to him motivated by the need to be politically correct more than scientifically rigorous, might be
reinforced by what happened when C.W. Mills published
The Sociological Imagination in 1959. He was attacked
for observing that young sociologists received little support for research involving variables unmeasurable in a
manner at least approaching conformity to the rules established by the natural sciences. Which meant in a
mathematical, or quantitative fashion. In Mills', estimation,
the reason for this orthodoxy had nothing to do with en-
hancing investigative rigor, and everything to do with dis-
couraging the pursuit of analyses disapproved of by the
ruling class. In particular, analyses of how power relationships actually operate in the United States, as opposed to
how young citizens are taught that they operate. This,
and many similar topics, did not lend themselves to quantitative analysis. Rather they involved what was called
qualitative analysis, which major sociology departments
frowned upon. Today, many studies in two subfields of
sociology, critical sociology and the sociology of knowledge, affirm that scholarship must always be held accountable as representing a search for knowledge rather
than the reinforcement of a prevailing convention. This is
the task of what is called the peer review system of science.

Unfortunately, numerous observations that Pinker did not
test his hypotheses so much as state them, or explain
why contrary views lacked credibility, seem valid. They

undermine his image as a courageous defier of conventionalism.

In Enlightenment Now, Pinker devotes 17 chapters to describing and documenting how people live longer than ever; how people live freer than ever of deadly disease; how we steadily sustain (feed) ourselves better than ever; how notwithstanding inequality, wealth grows and grows for nearly everyone; how today's least well off masses generally fare better than the most well off of the past; how serious environmental concerns verge on resolution through advanced science, technology, and management expertise; how peaceful relations among nations prevail more than ever in history; how people in general enjoy greater safety than ever from both natural and human threats; how terrorism constitutes more a nuisance than a threat to social stability; how in spite of some backsliding now and then democracy steadily increases as a dominant social force; how notwithstanding disturbing inequalities of wealth and opportunity, the principle that all people deserve human rights constantly advances; how knowledge essential to thriving grows both in quantity and quality; how the overall quality of life steadily increases, allowing people greater access to technological advances and the freedom to enjoy them; how despite the difficulty of rigorously defining happiness, its actual and potential growth clearly increases; how cataclysmic threats grow more apparent as technologies of knowledge improve, and more resolvable because of technologies of engineering; and finally, how the continued advance of progress seems well assured so long as humans can remain committed to Reason, Science, and Humanism, which are the titles of his final three chapters.

Pinker presents facts in support of the above assertions, and in refutation of imagined criticisms, all according to no stated criteria other than his own opinions concerning what is merits reportage and comment. He defends his thesis neither comprehensively nor rigorously. In neither volume does Pinker describe how Leviathan produces the positive effects he attributes to it — how it operates as molder and shaper of good social policy, how it wisely deals with bad social behavior, how it reinforces social stability. Nowhere does he explain in biological or psychological terms why absent Leviathan's control humans cannot collaborate effectively.

In the last three chapters, Pinker seems remarkably to abandon his thesis. Suddenly, responsibility for achieving social rationality falls upon the entire human community. He states passionately that people must embrace the principles of The Enlightenment in order for progress to continue. Reason, science, and humanism must become top priorities. And he expresses confidence that humans can step up to this challenge.

Making reason the currency of our discourse begins with clarity about the centrality of reason itself.... Humans may be vulnerable to bias and error, but clearly not all of us all the time... The human brain is capable of reason, given the right circumstance; the problem is to identify those circumstances and put them more firmly in place (Pinker, 2018, p. 375).

[Sadly] today the beauty and power of science are not just unappreciated but bitterly resented.... [Not least] by counter-culturalists and other liberals who view 'soul-less scientism' as oppositional to the esthetics and beauty of art and literature and in general to consideration of the richer nuances of the human character (2018, pp. 385-89)

Concerning humanism, Pinker is hopeful.

Evolution helps explain another foundation of secular morality: our capacity for sympathy... [E]volutionary psychology explains how it comes from the emotions that make us social animals...from the overlap in genetic makeup that interconnects us in the great web of life...Evolution thus selects for the moral sentiments: sympathy, trust, gratitude, guilt, shame, forgiveness, and righteous anger. With sympathy installed in our psychological makeup, it can be expanded by reason and experience to encompass all sentient beings (2018, p. 215).

In stark contrast with his strong emphasis on the savagery of ancient humans in Better Angels, Pinker now asserts that empathy, altruism, and affect regulation characterized our hunter-forager ancestors. In the final analysis, rather than defend elitism, he opens the door to whole-society discussion concerning how best to achieve sound social reasoning --particularly since now more than ever the survival of humans and other species depends upon it. In Rationality (2021), he devotes more than 300 pages to this assertion.

A major theme of this book is that none of us, thinking alone, is rational enough to consistently come to sound conclusions: rationality emerges from a community of reasoners ... (p.xvi).

On the final page of Enlightenment Now Pinker acknowledges that

...[m]uch suffering remains, and tremendous peril. But ideas on how to reduce them have been voiced, and an infinite number of others are yet to be conceived.... [T]here is no limit to the betterments we can attain if we continue to apply knowledge to enhance human flourishing (2018, p. 453).

Section IV: The Future

Part 14: The Power of Human Nature

<u>To recap and expand a little on the foregoing</u>

Cave paintings and other archaeological evidence, and research in evolutionary biology, psychology, modern psychology, and neuroscience tell us that our big-brained, language-sophisticated, immensely clever ancestors met ecological challenges with remarkable adaptivity for more than a hundred millennia. Unlike robotically altruistic ants and termites, humans could be driven by selfish as well as altruistic instincts, and manage the conflict between them. They could collaborate more effectively than any other creature. They could maximize the wisdom of their entire community rather than be forced to rely upon the wisdom of a single alpha leader-dominator, as did other apes. These attributes made them strong enough to eliminate all competitors, but warfare among them mostly ceased. It was more cost-effective to cooperate than to fight when one's competitors were as strong as oneself.

Our ancestors kept their hunting-foraging bands small enough not to overstress their ecological niches. Bands split when they became too big. What our ancestors failed to figure out, was how as a species not to overpopulate the large geographical areas that contained their niches. About twelve millennia ago, mainly to avoid conflict, most humans turned from nomadic hunting and foraging to sedentary farming. A few took up nomadic pastoralism and some of these began to specialize in warfare. Farming had long been part of humans' repertoire but was rarely employed. It produced a far less healthy diet. As things turned out, it did not even reduce conflict for long.

Bands and tribes amounting to a few hundred people settled around fertile land areas and built villages. Farming involved many specialized tasks not involved in hunting and foraging. A new occupation arose that involved coordinating these tasks. Sociologists called this managing the division of labor in society. Villagers chose people they often called chiefs to take on this challenge. The title usually implied respect rather than power. Some successful villages probably were ruled by chiefs, just as some hunter-forager bands before the agricultural revolution were alpha-male-dominated. For the most part, though, egalitarianism characterized our ancestors for several thousand years after the agricultural revolution, just as it mainly characterized them before it. In most villages, bands and tribes controlled social policy.

Farming was so labor-intensive that birth rates increased rapidly. As villages expanded in size, the distance between villages shrank. Suddenly cities containing thousands of people sprang into existence. New jobs arose and the division of labor increased. Overcrowding caused diet-based illnesses to spread and crime rates to increase. Armed conflicts with pastoralists over land management grew frequent. All of these factors contributed to chiefs needing to take on more responsibility and to be given more authority. It is likely that they also contributed to a lessening of band and tribal involvement in directing chiefs and holding them accountable. As full-fledged city managers, chiefs gained full control over the grain surpluses of cities (their wealth) as well as their military and police forces. For several thousand years chiefs employed their power in service of their communities. Archaeologists tell us that they did not strive to live better than others as payment for their services.

At a certain point, this changed. Chiefs became rulers and egalitarianism collapsed. Cities became city-states, city-states grew into empires, and warfare became not something to avoid or defend against, but to pursue. The urban community split into segments: a small united ruling class and a massive lower class subdivided into labor groups. Individuals competed with one another for earnings and other rewards. Obedience to ruling class authority took precedence over tribal loyalties. How this transition from democracy to autocracy occurred remains unclear, but research into how it has impacted humanity for the last five to seven millennia steadily grows. Hunter-foragers' joy of living within nature gave way to imperialists' drive to dominate and control nature. The Industrial Revolution accentuated and accelerated this trend. It produced significant technological advances at a high environmental cost --up until the present day.

It appears that elites' fear of vulnerability should they demonstrate openness to collaborating with the lower classes of their societies has always undermined social adaptivity and progress. Virtually every important innovation in modern history originated among the non-elite. In The Post American World, published in 2008, political analyst Fareed Zakaria echoed concerns published by Max Weber in 1897, Vilfredo Pareto in the early 1900s, and Erich Fromm in 1970, all scholars of great note, concerning how monarchs sought to hold onto to dominance of their society at all costs, even when this proved to be suicidal. Zakaria viewed the behavior of the U.S. power elite as no different. it seemed to evidence a kind of uncontrolled paranoia, a fatal loss of rationality.

Concern that elitism might be dysfunctional drove U.S. college students (and ultimately a global community of their peers) to embrace the writings of C. Wright Mills, Herbert Marcuse, and others during the 1960s and '70s. They created activist movements targeting the apparent incompetence of power elites to manage society, not just their inhumanity and greed. Since then, activism in pursuit of better social decision-making has continued to develop. But it has not yet gelled into a massive movement capable of reversing governmental policies and corporate practices that threaten social stability. They also threaten the continued existence of life on Earth.

E.O. Wilson's conclusion that humans must functionally address their damaging effects upon the biosphere immediately, is now shared by the vast majority of the scientific community. In his 2020 documentary, "A Life on Our Planet," natural historian David Attenborough presents some of the evidence that supports this consensus in a way all citizens can understand. He also notes that U.S. and other Western Empire policymakers refuse to acknowledge and respond to the science. Very simply, humans have virtually destroyed the biodiversity of the planet. Nearly all wildlife has been replaced by domesticated plants and animals, causing rampant deforestation. As a measurable result of this, global warming and oxygen depletion already approach levels associated with previous mass extinction events. All five destroyed a large percentage of life on the planet. Fortunately, the social transformations required to reverse this outcome are well within the means of humanity to accomplish, without undue hardship for anyone. Advanced technologies of engineering and communication assure this so long as they are brought to bear on the issue.

What comes next?

Many volumes recommending how to address aspects of the problems described by Attenborough exist — the need to reframe this or that policy, to employ this or that technology, to prioritize this or that specific goal. Herbert Marcuse, in his 1941 essay, Reason and Revolution, implied that such recommendations place the cart before the horse. They avoid the most critical issue: how to ensure that ideas addressing important challenges constitute the best reasoning society can produce. If hunter-forager bands and tribes produced better social reasoning, it is not because they were less complex than modern societies, in Marcuse's estimation, but because they were more egalitarian. In agreement with Georg W. Hegel and Karl Marx, Marcuse perceived that both as individuals and as communities, humans self-actualize the most fully, and are the happiest when applying their ability to think, feel and imagine freely and spontaneously. Such freedom must be tangible. It cannot just be idealized, as Hegel advocated.

In Eros and Civilization (1955), Marcuse rejected Hegel's premise that establishing democracy was beyond human capability. Marcuse perceived that people's craving for happiness through collaboration as equals constituted a powerful emotional drive inherent in the species. No ruling State was necessary, and it certainly was not desirable. Without referring to Emile Durkheim, he asserted that human society, whether simple or complex, operates most functionally when defined by the criteria that Durkheim called organic solidarity. Marcuse predicted that people would always seek to bring this about.

Marcuse was aware, however of a possible social pathology that might weigh against his premise. This was what his Frankfurt School colleagues Theodore Adorno and Erich Fromm called authoritarianism. Adorno described its psychological attributes in The Authoritarian Personality (1950), and Fromm revealed its sociological consequences in Escape From Freedom (1970) -- as noted previously. Essentially, these amounted to an entrenched set of cultural norms that prioritized obedience to authority over self-actualization. This was not the same thing as totalitarianism, where people were forced into obedience. Authoritarianism meant people's willing acceptance of rulership that required passive conformity. Authoritarianism also meant that rulers were unable to prioritize real social needs over their paranoid need to retain power at all costs even when this meant their own destruction. Authoritarianism dominated sociological thinking during the mid-twentieth century despite criticisms that Adorno's analysis lacked methodological rigor.

One manifestation of authoritarianism was what Durkheim called anomie, a profound sense of social disconnection accompanied by anxiety and depression, often resulting in suicide. Another was what Karl Marx called

alienation, a devaluing of oneself and one's labor in obedience to the norms of mechanical solidarity. It also
caused the devaluation of others. It reinforced fascism.
Fromm hoped that Marcuse's faith in 1960s activism in
the United States was justified but did not share his degree of optimism. Eventually, Marcuse came to wonder
whether his colleague might be right. Perhaps people
were too damaged by several millennia of authoritarianism to cope with the devices of modern oppression, such
as the psychological manipulations described by Antonio
Gramsci in The Prison Notebooks, noted in part 10. This
concern still occupies social psychologists.

A 1997 study by Bernard Lefkowitz, titled Our Guys: the
Clear Ridge Rape and the Secret Life of the Perfect Suburb, asked how a group of ideal young men, athletic stars
of their upper-class community, could have imagined that
gang-raping a fellow student was not only allowable but
appropriate. She was not of their social class, not one of
their peers, and she suffered from mild mental retarda-
tion. She'd developed a crush on one of the boys who
spoke with her on occasion, and seemed kind and caring.
When he invited her to a party in the basement of his
house, she readily agreed. When it all came to light, and
the school principal confronted and sanctioned them, the
boys expressed outrage at the punishment they received.
They were genuinely baffled by it. Lefkowitz sought to
discover what kind of social milieu could have produced
such an anti-social orientation.

*The ruling clique of teenagers adhered to a code of be-
havior that mimicked, distorted and exaggerated the values of the adult world around them. These values
extolled 'winners' -- the rich businessmen, the esteemed
professionals, the attractive, fashion-conscious wives, the
high-achieving children. They denigrated the 'losers' --
the less affluent breadwinners, the decidedly dowdy
wives, the inconspicuous, bashful, ungainly kids...Adults
might have forestalled the unfolding tragedy in their*

town.. They could have provided an alternative model of behavior to youngsters, one that emphasized fairness, compassion, humanity, and decency" (p. 493).

In Born to Be Good (2009), Psychologist Dacher Keltner observed that

The percentage of Americans who trust their fellow citizens has dropped 15 percentage points in the past fifteen years. Many indicators of our culture's poor health -- increasing feelings of anomie, greater loneliness, the trend toward less happy marriages -- are on the rise...[Inaccurate] claims that humans are wired to pursue self-interest, to compete, and to be vigilant to the bad rather than the good, .. lie at the heart of the intellectual traditions that have shaped Western thought (Keltner, 2009, pp. 7-10).

Despite the power of such norms, Keltner and other psychologists and neuroscientists tend to reinforce Marcuse's perception that humans value and reach for what E.O. Wilson called a harmonious social contract. How greatly authoritarianism undermines this drive and how quickly people can heal from its effects, though, remain open questions (Wilson, 1978; Goleman, 2006; Cozolino, 2006; Siegel, 2010 and 2015).

No evidence suggests, however, that authoritarianism demolishes people's ability to deal with life-threatening crises, natural or human-made. Throughout history, communities faced with chaos and death at the hands of monarchs finally rebelled. Ruling classes' disregard of ecological trends may now amount to just such a crisis. Massive public acceptance of authority could amount to passengers watching quietly as the ship-of-humanity's admirals sail it onto the rocks when this is easily avoidable. For children of the wealthy, thriving in a world inhumane for most while comfortable for themselves disappears as a viable (if terrible) option. Opposing the rule of their elders may be the only way to have a future at all. For children of the middle and lower classes, acquiescing to oppression in exchange for a measure of thriving also won't continue to work. Accommodation may be far more dangerous than defiance. Even the United State's overwhelming military supremacy as a guarantor of lifestyle advantages for its citizens at the expense of other nations' citizens no longer has any meaning. According to Immanuel Wallerstein (2003), the architect of World Systems Theory,

...the United States has been fading as a global power since the 1970s... The United States will continue to decline as a decisive force in world affairs over the next decade (pp.13-15)...The world revolution of 1968 was triggered by the discontents of all those who had been left out in the well-organized world order of U.S. hegemony (p50)...When the United States successfully made the first atomic bombs in 1945, it was determined to maintain a monopoly on such weapons...[Today] we are not sure how many countries have some capacity, even a considerable capacity...(p. 207

As indicated in part 11, the United State's upper-class can also no longer protect itself from lower-class outrage by oppressing one group of its citizens in favor of another, without heavy consequences. Social activism against racism and other forms of discrimination will not be easily crushed. Attempts to crush them will likely produce social chaos, at a time when chaos would fatally undermine efforts to avoid a sixth global extinction event. As Erich Fromm observed, when some citizens accept well-being based on the suppression of other citizens, this only reinforces the paranoid dysfunctionality of the ruling class that encourages and enables such inhumanity (1970).

The myth of Have supremacy

Unfortunately, a widespread public misperception seems to reinforce ruling class hegemony. Recently, The New York Times empaneled a prestigious group of journalists with particular expertise in environmental affairs. Their concern was that politics as usual may be unable to address the threat of potential eco-collapse brought about by human overpopulation and poor policymaking. The panelist who concluded the discussion observed:

And no matter what happens, there will be a class of people, all over the planet, who will have the money, the political connections, the insurance to move their houses inland or up the hill or whatever. And who knows, maybe the kind of thinking that we had in the United States back in the 1970s, about the population explosion and the need to control the global population, could make a return. You know, who cares if there is a winnowing out of global humanity if Noah's ark can be made available for the rich (Klein, 2021)?

In other words, many people assume that the United States, along with its allies, will probably address the impending ecological extinction event by seeking to shrink global population. This might well work, according to scientists, if it could be quickly accomplished. Which it could not be, in a humane fashion. Therefore they advise their government to reach out to Third World citizens with economic aid and technical assistance, and Third worlders to curtail their demands to partake of the good life of capitalism for a while longer. Many U.S. citizens perceive that their ruling class understands and rejects this advice, in favor of a different approach: the forcible reduction of planetary citizenship.

In 1952, French demographer Alfred Sauvy perceived that the Cold War following WWII, described in part 9, produced three groups of nations: the First World nations of the West, the Second World nations of the defeated Warsaw Pact, and nations a part of neither coalition, the Third World. These included much of Africa, Asia, Latin America, and Oceania, the great Island nations of the planet. Third World inhabitants wound up living under the First World's thumb, greatly lacking access to goods, services, ownership of property and other kinds of wealth, and personal and communal autonomy in general. Until a few decades ago, when rapid changes began to occur. Their command of knowledge and technology grew dramatically, and their craving for greater autonomy. Today Third World citizens seek full ownership of their natural resources and control over how they exploit them. The United States and other great powers, however, only increase their efforts to restrain such drives. This conflict rarely gains mention on the nightly news but receives significant attention from respected scholars (Frankopan, 2016 and 2018; Zakarias, 2008; Wallerstein 2003: Chomsky, 2003; Labeviere, 2000; among many others). Nor has it escaped public awareness.

Discussions with more than two thousand students of sociology over the past decade, from all demographics, inform me that the prestigious journalist was right about most of them. Their assumption concerning ruling class intentions influences how they define themselves politically. In none of my classes have the majority doubted that U.S. military force can, and will, deny access to third-world citizens, especially third-world citizens of color, who bang too vigorously upon the door of Western Empire for acceptance and inclusion. This includes not just people defined as militants and terrorists, but families struggling to survive. Most students find this potentiality heart-sickening and disgusting, but see little hope in pushing back against the in-humanism of their power elite. "Everyone is apathetic," is the comment I hear most often.

In response, I offer evidence supplied by scholars cited throughout this essay, among others, that First-World supremacy no longer exists in the way that it once did. Communities marked for exclusion from the "good life" of capitalism can now plausibly threaten mutually assured destruction -- "We can't defeat you, but we can create a state of chaos that envelopes us all." A genocidal U.S. initiative would ensure the certainty of a sixth planetary extinction event, at best. It might also produce nuclear winter on earth long before that. A good deal of pro-claimed apathy seems to dissolve during the course of this several-week presentation. Some students now view themselves as potential organizers. Many say they pos-sess an urge to organize but fear finding themselves alone. Most would like the opportunity to join a family-like movement they could trust. Most would like to be in-volved in the designing of actions, at some level.

In What's The Matter With Kansas (2004), Thomas Frank described how a powerful need for belonging, respect, and demographic prestige affected mostly rural, white, working-class Kansan's political orientation in a fashion similar to my student's professed apathy. Typically critical of the upper class in the past, often aggressively so, now they embraced their exploiters in a manner he found alarming. When politicians in service of the ruling class dressed like they did, and vowed to reinstate cultural val-ues honoring the majority's color, religion, and down-to-earth workmanship, all the while promoting legislation that further degraded them, Kansans seemed to swallow such nonsense hook line and sinker. Frank ended his book observing that

Kansas is ready to lead us singing into the apocalypse. It invites us all to join in, to lay down our lives so that others might cash out at the top; to renounce forever our middle-American prosperity in pursuit of a crimson fantasy of middle-American righteousness (p. 251).

At a book signing, a participant wondered if maybe the people Frank described simply gave up on their dreams. They finally accepted that democracy did not include them. America was divided into nobles and peasants, just like any monarchy of old. But as members of the largest peasant demographic in the nation, loyalty to the ruling class would grant them preferential treatment. Or as one of my students expressed it: "They could become first-among-pissants." This made sense to me at the time. It was how white supremacy worked.

If many of my country-people expect that their government can and will simply eliminate people they define as inconvenient, including both third world have-nots and many of their fellow citizens of color, but take care of Kansans and others like them so long as they remain loyal, it makes even more sense to me a decade and a half later. But what happens when Frank's subjects receive too much evidence to ignore that those to whom they show allegiance possess no such power as they imagine? Evidence that they can only be safe by abandoning their contract with them? Will they ignore this evidence, truly deny it?

Frank's subjects were older and more culturally and occupationally entrenched than my mostly adolescent students. My students' identities tended to be more fluid and their access to social mobility through education potentially greater. Just by being in college, they possessed a sense of belonging to a community of progress. To many of Frank's subjects, on the other hand, rejecting authoritarian norms meant relegating themselves to the cultural bottom rung of American society, with no apparent support from anyone. Hopefully, as they begin to grasp what my students learn, most will eventually abandon authoritarianism no matter what they claim to believe, and how depressingly they view their prospects. The growth of a strong activist movement resembling Occupy Wall Street, owned by no political party, intent upon transforming society in a manner Kansans and their peers once hoped for, ready to embrace them, would help a great deal. In fact, the existence of such a movement may well be a necessary condition of future thriving. There are a great many Kansans in the United States -- and the world.

In conclusion

Toward addressing the question posed in the introduction to this essay, can humanity avoid its trajectory into ecological chaos, and if so how, this essay arrives at the following hypothesis: Institutionalized in-compassion damages social functioning in the most fundamental way. It renders society incapable of sound enough adaptive reasoning. Human beings' celebrated skill at collaborative decision making shrinks drastically when mechanical solidarity eclipses organic solidarity.

Almost two years after its first appearance, humans cope poorly with a devastating viral pandemic under the auspices of policymakers committed only to maintaining ruling class hegemony at all costs. As a collaborative global community, implementing the expertise of our most competent analysts, things would be undeniably better. This reasoning applies even more to avoiding the impending extinction event. By the time we start going extinct, it will be too late to change. The current pandemic needs to alarm us enough to tend to the business of thriving quickly enough to succeed.

And succeed we can. Science tells us that the huge social-structural adjustments required can occur fairly painlessly. Essential communication and engineering technologies exist. We are not yet too numerous. Plenty of food, water, and high ground exists. Organized social activism has evolved enormously since the mid-1960s. Tipping points in service of thriving have occurred throughout history. Descriptions of scary collaborations in the face of massive threats reveal how as people find courage, they also find joy. Stories abound of people never being happier than when bonded with their mates in life-threatening situations. Addressing the threat becomes an exciting adventure, facing hardship becomes pioneering, what makes us happy also makes us strong. This is human nature.

References

Alexander, Michelle. (2012). The New Jim Crow: Mass incarceration in the age of colorblindness. The New Press.

Andreski, Stanislav (ed). (1983). Max Weber On Capitalism, Bureaucracy, and Religion. New Age Books.

Arendt, Hannah. (1973). The Origins of Totalitarianism. Harcourt Brace Jovanovich.

Aronowitz, Stanley. (1996). The Death and Rebirth of American Radicalism. Routledge.

Attenborough, David. (2020). A Life on Our Planet. Altitude Film Entertainment; Netflix; Silverback Films.

Bauer, Susan. (2007). History of the Ancient World. W.W. Norton.

Belenky, Mary. (1986).Women's Ways of Knowing. Basic Books.

Bell, Derrick. (2004). Silent Covenants: Brown v. board of education and the unfulfilled hopes for racial reform.Oxford University Press.

Bellwood, Peter S. (2005). The First Farmers: the origins of agricultural societies. Blackwell Publications.

Benedict, Ruth. (1959). Patterns of Culture. Houghton Mifflin.

Bobbitt, Philip. (2008). Terror and Consent: The wars for the twenty-first century. Knopf.

Bond, Becky and Zack Exley. (2017). Rules for Revolutionaries: How big organizing can change everything. Chelsea Green Publishing.

Bottomore, T.B. (1996). Elites and Society. Hammondsworth, Penguin.

Bourdieu, Pierre. (1998). Acts of resistance : Against the new myths of our time. Polity Press.

Bowlby, John. (1980). Attachment and Loss. Harper Colophon Books.

Boyd, Robert. (2018). A Different Kind of Animal: How culture transformed our species. Princeton University Press.

Buss, David M. (2015). Evolutionary Psychology: The new science of the mind. Pearson.

Chomsky, Noam and Edward S. Herman. (1988). Manufacturing Consent: The political economy of the mass media. Pantheon Books.

Chomsky, Noam. (2003). Hegemony or Survival: America's quest for global dominance. Metropolitan Books.

Christian, David. (2018). Origin Story: A big history of everything. Little Brown.

Coser, Lewis. (1977). Masters of Sociological Thought. Harcourt Brace.

Cozolino, Louis. (2006). The Neuroscience of Human Relationships: Attachment and the developing social brain. Norton.

Dawkins, Richard. (1989). The Selfish Gene. Oxford University Press.

de Waal, Franz. (2019). Mama's Last Hug: Animal emotions and what they tell us about ourselves. Norton.

Deleon, David (ed.).(1994). Leaders from the 1960s: A biographical sourcebook of american activism. Greenwood press.

Diamond, Jared M. (2005). Guns, Germs, and Steel : The fates of human societies. Norton.

Diamond, Jared M. (2011). Collapse: How societies choose to fail or succeed. Penguin.

Domhoff, William G. (1970). The Higher Circles: The governing class in America. Random House.

Durkheim, Emile. (1948). The Division of Labor in Society (2nd ed.). Free Press.

Durkheim, Emile. (1951). Suicide. Free Press.

Eisler, Rianne. (1988). The Chalice and the Blade: Our history, our future. Harper & Row.

Engels, Friedrich. (1972). The Origin of the Family, Private Property, and the State. Pathfinder Press.

Fanon, Franz. (1961). The Wretched of the Earth. Grove Press.

Ferraro, Gary and Susan Andreatta. (2010). Cultural Anthropology: An applied perspective (8th ed.). Cengage Learning.

Fonagy, Peter. (2002). Affect Regulation, Mentalization, and the Development of the Self. Routledge.

Frank, Thomas. (2004). What's the Matter With Kansas: How Conservatives Won the Heart of America. Metropolitan Books.

Frankopan, Peter. (2016). The Silk Roads: A new history of the world. Knopf.

Frankopan, Peter. (2016). The Silk Roads: A new history of the world. Knopf.

Frankopan, Peter. (2018). The New Silk Roads: The Present and Future of the World. Booms Bury.

Fromm, Erich. (1966). Marx's Concept of Man. Ungar.

Fromm, Erich. (1970). Escape From Freedom. Avon.

Galbraith, John K. (1967). The New Industrial State.The New American Library, Inc.

Gladwell, Malcolm. (2000). The Tipping Point. Little Brown.

Goleman, Daniel. (1996). Emotional Intelligence: why IT can matter more than IQ. Bloombury pub.

Goleman, Daniel. (2006). Social Intelligence: The new science of human relationships. Bantam.

Goodwyn, Lawrence. (1978).The Populist Moment: A short history of the agrarian revolt in America. Oxford University Press.

Gore, Al. (2000). An Inconvenient Truth: The crisis of global warming. Rodale Press.

Graeber, David and David Wengrow. (2021). The Dawn of Everything: A New History of Humanity. Farrar, Straus & Giroux.

Greider, William. (1987). Secrets of the Temple: How the Federal Reserve runs the country. Simon and Schuster.

Greider, William. (1992). Who Will Tell the People: The betrayal of american democracy. Simon & Schuster.

Hammond, Peter B. (1971). An Introduction to Cultural and Social Anthropology. McMillan.

Harari, Yuval. (2015). Sapiens: A brief history of human kind. Harper.

Hare, Paul. (1976). Handbook of Group Dynamics. Free Press.

Harman, Chris. (2008). A People's History of the World: From the stone age to the new millennium. Verso.

Haviland, William A. et. al. (2011). Cultural Anthropology: The human challenge. Wadsworth Cengage Learning.

Heilbroner, Robert. (1961). The Worldly Philosophers: The Lives and Times of the Great Economic Thinkers. Simon and Schuster.

Hobsbawm, Eric. (1962). The Age of Revolutions: 1789-1848. Weidenfeld and Nicolson.

Hobsbawm, Eric. (1975). The Age of Capital: 1848-1875. Weidenfeld and Nicolson.

Hobsbawm, Eric. (1987). The Age of Empire: 1875-1914. Weidenfeld and Nicolson.

Hobsbawm, Eric. (1994). The Age of Extremes: 1914-1991. Michael Joseph and Pelham Books.

Hofstadter, Richard. (1955).The Age of Reform. Vintage Books.

Hofstadter, Richard. (1965). The American Political Tradition and the Men Who Made it. Knopf.

Hunter, Herbert M. And Sameer Y. Abraham (eds.). (1987). Race, Class, and the World System: The sociology of Oliver Cox. Monthly Review Press.

Jahren, Hope. (2020). The Story of More: How we got to climate change and where to go from here. Vintage Press.

Johnson, Chalmers. (2001). Blowback: The Costs and Consequences of American Empire. Metropolitan Books.

Kauffman, L.A. (2017). Direct Action: Protest and the reinvention of american radicalism. Verso.

Keltner, Dacher. (2009). Born To Be Good: The science of a meaningful life. Norton.

Klein, Ezra. (2021). What if American Democracy Fails the Climate Crisis. The New York Times Magazine, July 27 2021. https://www.nytimes.com/2021/06/22/magazine/ezra-klein-climate-crisis.html

Kolko, Gabriel. (1962). Wealth and Poverty in America. Praeger.

Labeviere, Richard. (2000). Dollars for Terror: The United States and Islam. Algora Publishing.

La Feber, Walter. (1984). Inevitable Revolutions: The United States in Central America. W.W. Norton & Co.

Lefkowitz, Bernard. (1997). Our Guys: the clear ridge rape and the secret life of the perfect suburb. University of California Press.

Lewis-Kraus, Gideon. (2021, November 1). Early Civilizations Had it All Figured. The New Yorker.

Loewen, James. (1995). Lies My Teacher Told Me: Everything your american history text got wrong. New Press.

Machiavelli, Nicollo. (1999). The Prince. Penguin Books.

Mann, Charles. (2011).1493: Uncovering the new world Columbus created. Knopf.

Marcuse, Herbert. (1969). An Essay On Liberation. Beacon Press..

Marcuse, Herbert. (1972). One Dimensional Man. Abacus.

Marcuse, Herbert. (1974). Eros and Civilization. Beacon.

Marcuse, Herbert. (2000). Reason and Revolution (2nd edition). Routledge.

Marx, Karl. (1976). Capital: A critique of political economy, volume one. Penguin Books.

Maslow, Abraham. (1970). Motivation and Personality. Harper & Row.

McChesney, Robert. (1999). Rich Media, Poor Democracy. University of Illinois Press.

McLellan, David. (1976). Karl Marx. Penguin Books.

McLellan, David. (1979). Marxism After Marx. Houghton Mifflin.

Mills, C. Wright. (1956). The Power Elite. Oxford.

Mills, C. Wright. (1959). The Sociological Imagination. Oxford.

Mills. C. Wright. (1960). Letter to the New Left. New Left Review, No. 5, September-October 1960. https://www.marxists.org/subject/humanism/mills-c-wright/letter-new-left.htm

Mooney, Michael M. (1980). The Ministry of Culture. Wyndham books.

Palmer, R.R. & Joel Colton. (1971). A History of the Modern World. Alfred Knopf.

Pareto, Vilfredo. (1991).The Rise and Fall of Elites. Routledge.

Peck, James (ed.) (1987). The Chomsky Reader. Pantheon Books.

Phillips, Kevin. (1999). The Cousins Wars: Religion, politics, and the triumph of Anglo America. Basic Books.

Piketty, Thomas. (2014). Capital in the Twenty-first Century. The Belnap Press of Harvard University Press.

Pinker, Steven. (2011). The Better Angels of Our Nature: Why violence has declined. Viking.

Pinker, Steven. (2018). Enlightenment Now: The case for reason, science, humanism, and progress. Penguin Books.

Pinker, Steven (2021). Rationality: what it is, why it seems scarce, why it matters. Viking.

Roediger, David. (2005). Working Toward Whiteness: How america's immigrants became white. Basic Books.

Roszak, Theodore. (1969). The Making of a Counter Culture: Reflections on the Technocratic Society and its Youthful Opposition. Anchor Books.,

Schell, Jonathan. (1982). The Fate of the Earth. Knopf.

Schore, Alan. (1994). Affect regulation and the Origin of the Self. L. Erlbaum Associates.

Seppala, Emma and Kim Cameron. (2015, Dec. 1). Proof that positive work cultures are more productive. Harvard Business Review.

Siegel, Daniel. (2010). Mindsight: The new science of personal transformation. Random House Publishing Group.

Siegel, Daniel. 2015) Brainstorm: The Power and Purpose of the Teenage Brain. Penguin Publishing Group.

Sjoberg, Gideon.(1960).The PreIndustrial City: past and present. Free Press.

Stiglitz, Joseph. (2003). Globalization and Its Discontents. Norton.

Stone, Merlin. (1976). When God Was a Woman. Barnes & Nobles Books.

Surowiecki, James. (2004).The Wisdom of Crowds. Doubleday.

Wallerstein, Immanuel. (2003). The Decline of American Power. New Press.

Ward, Brian (ed.). (2010). The 1960s: A documentary reader. Wiley-Blackwell.

Weber, Max. (2013). The Agrarian Sociology of Ancient Civilizations. Verso.

Welker, B. H. (2017, July 10). The History of Our Tribe: Hominini. Open Textbook Library, https://open.umn.edu/opentextbooks/textbooks/467

Weinstein, James. (1968). The Corporate Ideal in the Liberal State: 1900-1918. Beacon.

Williams, William Appleman. (1961). Contours of American History. World Publishing Co.

Wilson, Edward O. (1975). Sociobiology. Belknap Press of Harvard University Press.

Wilson, Edward O. (1978). What is Human Nature. Harvard University Press.

Wilson, Edward O. (1998). Consilience: The Unity of Knowledge. Alfred A. Knopf.

Wilson, Edward O. (2019). Genesis: The deep origin of societies. Liverwright.

Wise Bauer, Susan. (2007).The History of the Ancient World: From the earliest accounts to the fall of Rome. W.W. Norton.

Woodward, C. Vann. (1974). The Strange Career of Jim Crow. Oxford University Press.

Zakaria, Fareed. (2008).The Post American World. W.W. Norton & Co.

Zinn, Howard. (1980). A People's History of the United States. Harper Collins.

Acknowledgements

I am so grateful for the support and guidance of my partner, loving critic and spouse of 57 years, Shula Weiner; for the best editing in the universe by Melanie Weiner; for the most compassionate and helpful readers one could hope for, Arielle Cernes, Tyson McLeod, David Gardner, Joe Manning, and Carl Pickhardt; for the superb copy editing of Beryl Knifton; for the many students who pointed out sections needing work as well as those they found especially valuable; and for the invaluable mentorship of my publisher, Bill Benitez.

www.ingramcontent.com/pod-product-compliance
Lightning Source LLC
Chambersburg PA
CBHW050120280326
41933CB00010B/1184